FERRARI
512 S/M

1970 onwards (all models)

Dedication

First published in August 2016

A catalogue record for this book is available from the British Library.

ISBN 978 0 85733 787 0

Library of Congress control no. 2015958626

Published by Haynes Publishing,
Sparkford, Yeovil,
Somerset BA22 7JJ, UK.
Tel: 01963 440635
Int. tel: +44 1963 440635
Website: www.haynes.co.uk

Haynes North America Inc.,
861 Lawrence Drive, Newbury Park,
California 91320, USA.

Printed in Malaysia.

Emanuele 'Elio' Nicosia
11 January 1953–23 March 2016

As this book was nearing submission date, I received the terribly sad news that someone who I frequently consulted and greatly admired, Emanuele Nicosia, had passed away. Born in Catania, Sicily, 'Elio' – as he was known to his friends – studied engineering at university there and participated in the Targa Florio in his modified Fiat 500. In 1976 he became the first Italian student to receive a Masters degree in Automotive Design at the RCA in London. This was followed by spells in the Ford Design Studio in the USA and then as a senior designer at Pininfarina before opening his own design studio in 1985. In 2010 Elio moved to Pune in India, where he lectured at the Centre for Automotive Design.

More times than I can remember, Elio has patiently explained complex design techniques to me, and issues relating to vehicle aerodynamics. Whether in Italy or in India, he was always willing to help, no matter how busy he was. His willingness to explain some aerodynamic issue or share his love for motor racing back in the '70s was infectious, and it was my privilege to be on the receiving end of his enthusiasm on numerous occasions.

In April 2015 he was diagnosed with cancer, and, following surgery, returned to his home in Catania to continue his recuperation. However, less than a year after the initial diagnosis, Elio passed away in intensive care at the Militello in Val di Catania, close to his family and home. Elio loved playing music and cooking, but above all he loved life, teaching, and helping people. He will be sadly missed.

FERRARI 512 S/M

1970 onwards (all models)

Owners' Workshop Manual

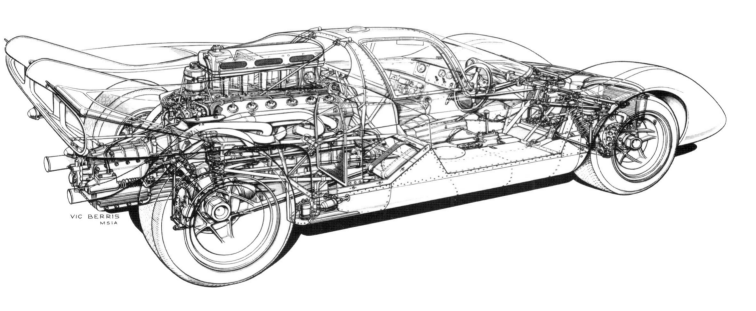

VIC BERRIS
MSIA

An insight into the design, engineering, maintenance and operation of Ferrari's iconic 1970s sports racing car

Glen Smale

Contents

6   Introduction

8   The Ferrari 512 story

The motor racing scene in 1969   10
Racing in 1970   13
Racing in 1971   31
Motor racing summary   48

50   Anatomy of the Ferrari 512

Body and design   54
Chassis   66
Engine   68
Cooling system   75
Transmission   76
Steering and suspension   79
Brakes   81
Wheels and tyres   83
Interior   84
Fuel tanks   87
Lamps and lighting   89
Electrical   90

92   The engineer's view

Running a Ferrari 512 S and 512 M in period   94
Running a Ferrari 512 S today   105

112   The owner's view

The Sunoco 512 S   115
Nick Mason gives his views on 512 ownership   117
Values   120

126   The driver's view

Sam Posey (NART)   128
Mario Andretti from behind the wheel of a 512 S   131
Derek Bell from behind the wheel of a 512 S   132
Driving a Ferrari 512 today   137

140   The Ferrari 512 S and 512 M chassis record

Individual chassis numbers   142
Conclusion   153

154   Index

OPPOSITE The #7 factory entered Ferrari 512 S driven by Derek Bell/Ronnie Peterson speeds past the pits during the 1970 Le Mans 24-Hour race, with the Mike Parkes/Herbert Muller Scuderia Filipinetti 512 S in close pursuit. *(LAT)*

BELOW The engine of Nick Mason's Ferrari 512 S (chassis 1026). *(Author)*

The Sam Posey/Ronnie Bucknum #11 NART Ferrari 512 S finished fourth in 1970 Le Mans 24-Hour race. The #10 NART/Gelo Racing Team 512 S of Helmut Kelleners/Georg Loos is behind. *(LAT)*

Introduction

At the mere mention of the name Ferrari today, whether at a race meeting, in a coffee shop or just a casual gathering of friends, ears prick up and huddles tighten as the discussion begins. Back in the 1970s too, support for Ferrari was almost feverish, and there was little that the Italian manufacturer could do wrong. Their GT cars were clinically efficient in winning, with looks that few road car manufacturers could match. On the racetrack, Ferrari's sports cars were awesome in the full meaning of the word, commanding fear and respect from all sides.

When the 512 S was introduced in 1970 the racing world fully expected it to dominate straight out of the box, but their old rival Porsche already had a foot up on the podium with their 917. Ferrari's experience and racing knowhow suggested that the 512 S would deliver the victories that Ferrari had become used to, but testing of this newcomer had been limited due to the difficult winter of 1969. Nevertheless, such was the universal respect for Ferrari that even the underperforming 512 S could never be ruled out on race day, as a podium finish on its first outing and victory in its second race bore testament.

While the factory only participated with the 512 S officially in 1970, it was the privateers who carried the flag for the Italian manufacturer for 1970 and 1971 and beyond. The 512, in either S- or M-spec, certainly gave the Porsches a good run for their money, as witnessed by the Penske Sunoco Ferrari 512 M, which took pole position at both the Daytona and Sebring races in 1971. But ultimately the lack of development and testing by the factory was the difference between the Porsches and the Ferraris. Despite its lack of overall victories, the 512 is still celebrated as one of Ferrari's most loved and admired sports racers. It posed a very real threat wherever and whenever it participated because it was capable of beating its contemporary opposition.

This book looks at the car's competition history, its design and the mechanical details that made it such a feared racer. We have been fortunate enough to speak with the Ferrari engineer responsible for bringing the 512 to life, as well as some of those who prepared the cars for racing and drove them. We have also been fortunate enough to interview some 512 owners, both contemporary and current, and have included a valuable commentary on the state of the current Ferrari 512 market values. This book is consequently suitable for all levels of interest, from the newest enthusiast to the most ardent supporter.

Acknowledgements

When I undertook to write this book on the Ferrari 512 S and M, I was blissfully unaware of the complexities that contributed to this great racer. It was for this reason that I embarked on a campaign to seek out those who were involved with it in some way during its evolution and heyday. The list of willing, eager and enthusiastic helpers is a long one, and it would be impossible to provide full details of how each of them helped, but they will know who they are, and I thank every one of them for their gifts of time and knowledge.

Having access to a Ferrari 512 was made possible by the very willing Nick Mason, where Charles, Ben and Mike answered countless questions. In the same vein, I must thank Gregor Fisken for so generously allowing me to photograph the 512 M, and to Rory Henderson and Riiko Nüüd for their assistance too. When I asked Martin Raffauf if he knew anyone who could help me from the 1970s, he gave me one name, Judy Stropus, who proceeded to open the floodgates to so many people that I was unable to contact all of them. Of course, I have interviewed Derek Bell, Brian Redman and Mark Hales on a number of occasions before, and their contributions were once again greatly appreciated. Also from behind the wheel, Mario Andretti, Sam Posey and David Hobbs gave enthusiastic accounts of what the car was like to drive in period.

As team members, Don Cox, Dan Luginbuhl, Woody Woodard, Kirk White, Dick Fritz and François Sicard provided invaluable insights into the preparation and maintenance of the Ferraris in period. Sadie Chapple, Amy Christie and Max Girardo from RM Sotheby's contributed in a significant way, and Stephen Lay of Maranello Concessionaires was once again extremely kind and helpful. I was especially grateful to my late, great friend, Elio Nicosia, who introduced me to Mauro Forghieri. I would also like to thank Bob Houghton for his help in answering the many questions that I had. On the photographic side I would like to mention Tim Wright, John Brooks, Simon Hildrew, Peter Collins, Mike Hayward, Trevor Swettenham (BARC) and RM Sotheby's.

Finally, a really big thank you to my wife, Elke, who has sifted through and prepared many of my own photos for this book. This has been a huge task, spread over many weekends and late nights over the past few months.

Glen Smale
May 2016

'The prospect of a confrontation between the sports giants using such state-of-the-art weapons was quite enticing. That the reality didn't quite match the expectation isn't nearly as important as the fact that the contest elevated this division of the sport to the highest level of interest it had ever known.'

— János Wimpffen

Chapter One

The Ferrari 512 story

Enzo Ferrari was probably quite annoyed with himself that he misjudged Porsche's entry into Group 4 racing as it was in 1969, and so a plan was hastily put in place to remedy this the following year. The result was an intoxicating recipe for one of the greatest showdowns in motor racing. History reveals, though, that while this clash of titans didn't quite turn out as he had hoped, the Ferrari 512 – in either S- or M-spec – still raises the hairs on the back of one's neck as much today as it did at the time.

OPPOSITE NART Ferrari 512 S chassis 1006.
(Don Heiny, courtesy of RM Sotheby's)

The motor racing scene in 1969

Motor racing is all about innovation, and after the decade of the 1960s during which the sport took some giant and memorable steps forward, the authorities were looking to consolidate that progress and to bring everyone back into order. Porsche had been steadily making inroads into the top echelons of the sport with their 'plastic' racers, while the world had witnessed the Shelby Cobra's meteoric rise to significance when it wrestled the GT Manufacturers' Championship away from Ferrari. Ford had seen that Ferrari could be beaten as its mighty GT40, in its various forms (Ford GT40 Mk I, Mk II and Mk IV), took the honours at Le Mans for four successive years between 1966 and 1969.

The motor sport authorities sought to cater for two classes – Group 4 and Group 6 – in the world of sports car racing. Group 4 would consist of those cars which raced in 1968, and required a minimum of 50 units to be manufactured in 12 consecutive months. For the 1969 season the production requirement was lowered from 50 units to just 25; then for the 1970 and 1971 seasons the old Group 4 class was renamed Group 5, and the existing rules and regulations were carried over from the old group to the new.

Group 6 cars were subject to the new 3-litre engine capacity limit that was the direction in which the Fédération Internationale de l'Automobile (FIA) – the international body that governed and regulated motor racing events – was hoping to drive the sport. While this may have sounded quite within the remit of many manufacturers, the time allowed in which to design, develop and test a new car to comply with this 3-litre limit just wasn't long enough. Making matters even more uncertain for the authorities, few manufacturers had the resources to react quickly enough and even fewer seemed willing to try.

In order to bolster potentially flagging grid numbers, the FIA relented and increased the engine capacity limit for Group 4 cars to 5 litres, which would allow some of the older models to be re-entered and basically receive a second lease of life. What the Commission Sportive Internationale (CSI) – which was at the time the FIA's independent competition arm – was hoping was that in this way cars such as the Ford GT40, Lola T70 coupé and Ferrari 250 LM would be encouraged back on to the grid. These hadn't actually been manufactured in sufficient quantity (50 units) to qualify for Group 4, but the CSI wanted to prevent them from going into early retirement, as despite being relatively old they still held some attraction for spectators. What the FIA didn't expect, though,

BELOW In 1965 the #7 Ferrari 250 LM driven by Mike Spence and John Love finished sixth in the Kyalami 9-Hour at Johannesburg, South Africa. *(Virtual Motorpix)*

was to be presented with a batch of 25 newly designed and manufactured sports racing prototypes, as happened with the Porsche 917.

This loophole offered Ferdinand Piëch, head of research and development at Porsche, the perfect opportunity to develop his all-conquering race car that would finally allow him to lift the Le Mans 24-Hours trophy. The Porsche 917 caught the sporting authorities completely off guard, and frankly most of the race car manufacturing world as well.

Having been soundly beaten at Le Mans by Ford over the four preceding years, Enzo Ferrari wasn't about to let Porsche get one up on him as well, and so he set about creating his own challenger. The FIA were therefore confronted not only with the Porsche 917 in 1969, but with Ferrari entering the fray with a similar race car in 1970; but there was nothing that could be done to stop them as both cars fell within the regulations for that class. It is also feasible that the FIA considered a Porsche/Ferrari battle to be to their advantage, as it would be something that spectators would gladly pay to see.

However, the attitude of the CSI inspectors who attended the presentation of the Porsche 917s and subsequently arrived at the Ferrari factory to approve the 512s could not have been more different. When the inspectors arrived at the Stuttgart factory on 20 March 1969 they were presented with three fully assembled Porsche 917s with the balance in various stages of assembly. Sufficient sets of parts were present for the unfinished vehicles, bringing the potential total of completed cars to

25, Porsche arguing that they could easily build them if needed but would then have to take them apart again to prepare them for racing. The inspectors, however, refused to homologate the 917 on the grounds that they required all 25 cars to be fully assembled and working. The inspectors returned on 21 April to find all 25 cars complete, and, in an attempt to prove his point, Ferdinand Piëch invited the CSI team

BELOW Deep in discussion, the CSI delegation visits the Porsche factory for the second time on 21 April 1969. From left to right: Ferdinand Piëch, Herbert Staudenmaier, Dean Delamont, Herbert Schmitz and Helmuth Bott.
(Porsche-Werkfoto)

leader, Dean Delamont, to trial any of them. The invitation wasn't taken up.

This strict approach was somewhat unusual for the CSI, because in the past a manufacturer's word that the correct number would be produced was usually sufficient; and when the CSI inspectors arrived the following year to check on Ferrari 512 production, they apparently went away satisfied even though only 17 cars had been fully assembled – despite Enzo Ferrari's reputation for not producing all the cars required for homologation on previous occasions. The CSI's leniency, though, may have been due to the potential racing rivalry that would ensue on track, the financial benefits of which would outweigh the small issue of any production shortfall.

There is no doubt that not only had the CSI been caught by surprise with the Porsche 917, but so had Enzo Ferrari. All of this meant that Ferrari didn't have the right hardware available to just pull off the shelf, so he had to combine the lessons learned from the company's Can-Am escapades and its 312 P endeavours. Although Ferrari was a bit late in coming to the party, author János Wimpffen considered that: 'The prospect of a confrontation between the sports giants using such state-of-the-art weapons was quite enticing. That the reality didn't quite match the expectation isn't nearly as important as the fact that the contest elevated this division of the sport to the highest level of interest it had ever known.'

The Ferrari 512 was unveiled at the Turin Motor Show late in 1969. It was an aggressive-looking car, with a flat and wide body. Both the Porsche 917 and the Ferrari 512 had interchangeable short- and long-tail rear ends that could be used in accordance with the demands of the circuit. The first Ferrari model launched was the S (S = Sport), a 5.0-litre V12-engined sports car characterised by having twin low-level driving lights mounted in the centre of the nose section, with an air inlet slot on either side.

The 512 M (M = Modificato), introduced in time for the last event of the 1969 season at the Österreichring, had a revised nose section devoid of the central, low-level driving lights, having instead a full-width air intake. The 512

M then competed in the non-Championship 9-Hours race at Kyalami in South Africa, which it won. This introduction was timed to prepare the car for the 1970 season, and the Kyalami race served as the new model's test session. New for the 512 M was a centrally mounted airbox mounted atop the engine cover to scoop the air that flowed over the roof and direct it down into the engine bay to feed cool air to the carburettors. The M also benefitted from improved aerodynamics and better weight distribution.

The Porsche 917 and Ferrari 512 S are basically similar in that both are built around a tube-frame chassis structure. Development of the 512 started well after the Porsche 917, but was this because Ferrari wasn't prepared to build 50 Group 5 cars (later reduced to 25)? And what prompted Ferrari to change his mind? When asked, Mauro Forghieri, Ferrari's chief engineer, replied, 'It was partially because Ferrari wasn't prepared to build the required 50 cars, but also because we were so involved in Formula 1. After some discussion concerning our return to sports car racing we decided to return to this class, and development of the car started at the end of September 1969.'

Even though the 512 was more powerful than its German rival, the history books show that it lost out to the Porsche 917 in most of the races through the 1970 and 1971 seasons. With the benefit of hindsight, Forghieri explained why this might have been the case: 'Due to the late decision to proceed with the 512, we didn't have time for the usual wind tunnel tests. Road tests too weren't sufficient, and in Sicily the winter was very bad.'

Under Article 251 and Appendix J of the International Sporting Code 1969, the regulations governing entries in Group 4 of Category A required that just 25 race cars be produced. By definition, the number of cars produced under this code had to be manufactured within a period of 12 consecutive months. In the 1971 edition of the Sporting Code, the race cars previously classified as Group 4 were reclassified as Group 5. In addition, the minimum production clause now specified that the total production run of vehicles required for each class – 25 in the case of the Ferrari 512 – had to be complete

and ready to race upon inspection by the CSI. Unlike previous years, Article 252 (e) under Definitions and General Prescriptions was quite clear on this, emphasising that the vehicles had to be 'entirely finished' cars. No doubt the Porsche 917 and Ferrari 512 fiasco of 1969–70, where these manufacturers had taken advantage of a loophole in the regulations to develop completely new racing cars, was still fresh in the minds of the CSI officials.

When it was finally ready, the 512 S was introduced to the press at a conference on 6 November 1969 at the Gatto Verde restaurant, located in the foothills of the Apennines above Maranello. Present at the launch was the engineer responsible for the project, Mauro Forghieri, as well as Ferrari drivers Clay Regazzoni, Arturo Merzario and Ignazio Giunti.

Racing in 1970

During the 1969 season, Porsche had raced its new 4.5-litre 917 with varying success. Despite their early worries about

the car's stability at speed, they were able to boast at least one victory that year, at the Österreichring 1,000km on 10 August. The 917's first outing was at Spa on 11 May, but its handling was too wayward for even the masterful Jo Siffert and Brian Redman, who consequently reverted to the older Porsche 908L with which they won the race, beating the Ferrari 312 P in the process.

Subsequent 917 outings in 1969 included the Nürburgring 1,000km in June, and the Le Mans 24-Hour race the same month. By the time of the Le Mans race Porsche had polished many of the 917's rough edges, and this enabled Vic Elford to put the car on pole. Elford and Richard Attwood put in a truly startling performance, but while leading and with just 45 laps to go a clutch problem caused their retirement. At the last race of the year for the World Manufacturers' Championship, the Österreichring 1,000km in August, the 917 took its first win, in the hands of Jo Siffert and Kurt Ahrens. Attwood and Redman were third in another 917, and

ABOVE Luigi Chinetti's NART Ferrari 512 S chassis 1006.
(RM Sotheby's)

ABOVE Porsche 917 #29 driven by Jo Siffert/Kurt Ahrens crosses the finishing line for its maiden win at Zeltweg in Austria on 10 August 1969. *(Porsche-Werkfoto)*

no doubt the champagne corks popped with increased frequency that night.

Why was this important? Well, Ferrari was entering the Group 5 fight at the start of the following season with the 512 S. The problem for Ferrari was that Porsche had got a year of racing behind them with the 917 and, in the process, had ironed out many of the kinks in its armour. In addition, Porsche would put in

many miles of testing during the autumn and winter months of 1969 in preparation for the 1970 season; and John Wyer, who had won the 1968 and 1969 Le Mans 24-Hours with Ford, had been contracted to run the Porsche factory team. Combined with his military-style race team management and organisation, Wyer's experience would be felt by all of Porsche's competitors in the New Year, so Ferrari had every reason to be worried.

It was with no small effort on Ferrari's part that they managed to get five 512s to Daytona for the first race of the season, as a metal-workers' strike in Italy had seriously hampered the factory's production progress. Mauro Forghieri confirmed that 'Considerable industrial disruption delayed us on the design of the 512, because the draughtsmen and the mechanics were forced to stay out of the factory.'

The first race of the 1970 season, and the first round in the much-awaited Porsche versus Ferrari contest, was about to commence. Porsche not only had the benefit of a full year's competition experience, but their all-new team management was out of the top drawer. Ferrari, however, was renowned for pulling the proverbial rabbit out of the hat, and producing race-winning cars right out of the box. They also had the benefit of many years of race experience across numerous race classes, and an extremely impressive record of achievements. Of course, in Ferrari's favour

BELOW Spare engine cover panels for Ferrari works cars #26, #27 and #28 at the 1970 Daytona 24-Hours. *(LAT)*

too was that mystique that went with the name, which was itself worthy of note to the enthusiastic spectators who had paid money to sit in the stands. Porsche was nevertheless a factor to be reckoned with, because their reputation was one of clinical performance and solid reliability. The season looked to be a sizzler on paper, although in reality the outcome differed somewhat from expectations.

Clearly, after the 512 was victorious in only its second competitive outing – namely the Sebring 12-Hours – the future must surely have looked bright for the Ferrari racer. Forghieri explained why the 512 didn't achieve a higher record of wins: 'There were no developments on the car, and some areas of it weren't right. We had to do too much to increase power, because Ferrari back then wasn't the Ferrari of today.'

Daytona 24-Hours
31 January/1 February 1970

Luigi Chinetti, the eastern USA Ferrari distributor, established a race team that became well known internationally – the North American Racing Team, or NART. Dick Fritz, team manager for the NART team, remembers waiting for their first 512 S to arrive for the opening race of the season, the Daytona 24-Hours. It only arrived on the Monday of race week, which didn't leave the team much time, not only to get used to the newcomer but also to prepare it for the race.

Ferrari had clearly arrived at the party a bit late, which could imply that the 512 S wasn't their main focus of attention. While the factory didn't want to give this impression to its customers or the public, the truth of the matter wasn't far from this. In 1970, Ferrari engineers

BELOW The #25 NART 512 S driven by Dan Gurney/Chuck Parsons (chassis 1014) retired with gearbox problems in the 1970 Daytona 24-Hours. *(LAT)*

who would attend races included Gianni Marelli, Giacomo Caliri and Carlo Bussi, but being the 512's first competitive outing, chief engineer Mauro Forghieri was in attendance at Daytona.

The five 512s were flown into Daytona airport on a Canadair CL 44 swing-nose plane, three cars being for the factory, one for Chinetti and one for Picchio Rosso. Dick Fritz recalled: 'They got trucked in from the airport and Forghieri put them into the garages and closed the doors. I told him that I needed to get my car, but he said, "First we're going to have lunch, so come back after lunch."' So after lunch Fritz made his way back to the garages and Forghieri opened the doors to reveal the five 512s. Fritz asked which was their car, to which Forghieri replied that they were all the same, and so, pleased that he could take first pick, he said, 'OK, I will take that one.' 'No,' replied Forghieri, 'yours is over there,' which left Dick Fritz slightly puzzled as to why he had been given a choice in the first place.

Upon inspection, Fritz noticed that the Chinetti car had no roll bar and no seat belts. Looking somewhat concerned, Forghieri asked, 'Is there a problem?' Fritz proceeded to point out what was missing but Forghieri simply replied that Fritz would be able to sort that out easily, adding, 'We didn't have enough Carter fuel pumps so your car still needs some, but they are here in America, so you can just call them up and get some.'

Fritz noticed that the three factory cars were all fitted with roll bars and racing harnesses, but when challenged Forghieri shot back, 'Yes, we have roll bars and shoulder harnesses, but at Le Mans this isn't required.' Despite pointing out that they weren't racing at Le Mans that weekend, Dick Fritz realised that he wasn't going to win that argument.

The situation facing Dick Fritz was that he had very little time in which to get the 512 running, let alone prepared for racing. First he got Wayne Sparling, a local mechanic and fabricator, to make up a roll cage of sorts. Sparling used a 'bunch of exhaust tubing which he bought at the local auto parts store', as Fritz put it, and although this wasn't particularly fit for purpose it was the best that could be done in the available time. From this Sparling bent and welded the roll cage, which was then installed in the car along with the Carter fuel pumps that Fritz had acquired.

The seat belts required a rather more innovative approach. Fritz had rented a Mercury Cougar at the track, 'so we took the seat belts and shoulder harnesses out of that and made up the shoulder harnesses and seat belts for the Ferrari. Of course,' he added with a smile, 'we returned the rent-a-car without them.'

The #25 Chinetti Ferrari 512 S (chassis 1014), to be driven by Dan Gurney and Chuck Parsons, was fortunately ready in time for

BELOW The #30 Corrado Manfredini/ Gianpiero Moretti (chassis 1032) Picchio Rosso 512 S retired just past the halfway mark following an accident in the 1970 Daytona 24-Hours. *(LAT)*

practice and qualifying, and was placed sixth on the starting grid. Dick Fritz had no fewer than six cars running in the race: two 312 Ps, a 250 LM, a single 512 S, a 275 GTB/C and a 365 GTB/4 Daytona. The other 512s in the race were three factory cars crewed by Nino Vaccarella/Ignazio Giunti (#26), Jacky Ickx/Peter Schetty (#27) and Mario Andretti/Arturo Merzario (#28), and a Scuderia Picchio Rosso car driven by Corrado Manfredini/Gianpiero Moretti (#30).

Dick Fritz recounted how events unfolded: 'The first thing that happened was that Dan Gurney broke the shift lever off right under the shift knob. He came in and said, "The shift knob has gone, it's down there under the brake pedal. Are you going to fix it?" I said we would, so we took a rag and made a ball around the shift lever and taped it on, and it lasted for a number of hours.'

First of the Chinetti cars to bow out was the 365 GTB/4 Daytona because, as Fritz said, 'It was going through tyres so quickly that they didn't have enough.' The next Chinetti car out was the #20 275 GTB/C with an overheating problem on lap 308. Finally, the transmission of the 512 broke after 464 laps; but the two 312s and the 250 LM finished fourth, fifth and seventh respectively.

The two Gulf Porsches competing set the initial pace along with the Andretti Ferrari, but the 5-litre Ferraris proved the thirstier of the leading bunch. While the top teams took it in turns to have heart-stopping moments with wall-scraping incidents, the Ferraris seemed to have many small problems. When the Ickx/Schetty car dropped out because of an accident the Belgian transferred to Andretti's car, displacing Merzario. Despite qualifying the #28 factory 512 S on pole, Mario Andretti/Arturo Merzario finished in third place, albeit 48 laps adrift of the winning Porsche 917 K.

Two of the factory 512s were out of the running quite early on due to accidents, the #27 factory car of Ickx/Schetty on lap 115 and the #26 car of Vaccarella/Giunti after 89 laps. The #30 Scuderia Picchio Rosso of Manfredini/Moretti also succumbed to an accident on lap 412.

Although only one of the five 512s entered went the distance it was the factory car of Andretti/Merzario/Ickx that finished in third place. This at least left the Ferrari team with some level of confidence in their new sports racer for the future.

Sebring 12-Hours
21 March 1970

If the opening race of the season at Daytona had provided thrills and spills enough for the spectators, the second race at Sebring would end up being one of the most thrilling in memory. This time four 512 S cars lined up on the grid against an equal number of 917s, but it was the Italian car that would triumph on the

ABOVE Mario Andretti and Arturo Merzario (chassis 1026) put in a spirited performance in the #28 works car to finish third at Daytona in 1970, giving the 512 S its first podium. *(LAT)*

ABOVE On 21 March 1970 the Mario Andretti/Arturo Merzario pairing was in action again in the Sebring 12-Hours, driving the #19 works car (chassis 1010). When this car retired Andretti transferred to the #21 works car to win the race. *(LAT)*

Hendricks World War 2 airbase circuit in Florida. The win, though, would be a hard-fought affair, going right down to the wire with the German manufacturer – but not against the fearsome 917; instead it was the 908 stalwart of Steve McQueen and Peter Revson that almost upset the applecart.

Once again there were three factory 512s in the field, two of which were Spiders, although this term is slightly misleading as there was just a square panel missing in the cockpit roof. The two Spiders were driven by Andretti/Merzario (chassis 1010) and Ickx/Schetty (chassis 1012), while the Coupé was driven by Giunti/Vaccarella (chassis 1026).

The Chinetti 512 S still retained its exhaust-pipe roll cage, as according to Dick Fritz they didn't have time to change it between races with the number of cars that needed prepping. 'It was really well made, but then you could take anything and paint it black and it would look OK,' Fritz quipped. Chinetti took the opportunity to mix up the sports car and prototype drivers somewhat, and this saw Sam Posey partnered with Ronnie Bucknum in the 512 S for the Sebring race.

Pole position was taken by Mario Andretti in a time of 2:33.5, and for the first time a rolling start was used at Sebring. This favoured Andretti, who was used to this type of start procedure from Indianapolis racing, and at the fall of the

flag he made good time by getting away quicker than anyone else. Andretti held his lead and handed over to Merzario as planned, but then a five-car incident in the early stages dealt a severe blow to several top teams. Posey in the Chinetti/NART Ferrari 512 S made contact with a smaller car, which hampered the Ferrari's progress. As the race approached the halfway mark it was the three factory Ferraris that held positions 1-2-3, but this was not to last.

While the factory 512s of Ickx/Schetty and Giunti/Vaccarella were experiencing problems, the Andretti/Merzario Ferrari held a strong 11-lap lead into the second half of the race. Well into the final quarter of the race, Andretti brought the lead Ferrari into the pits with a gearbox problem, which, when Merzario took the wheel, promptly left him stranded out on the track. With less than an hour of the race left, Andretti was then drafted into the Giunti/Vaccarella car, which had had its suspension damage repaired and was maintaining fourth place.

It has been written by many a journalist that the last part of this race was one of the finest displays of sports car driving seen to date, and it was certainly Andretti's finest hour. He put in an inspirational spell of driving, and hauled in, then overtook, the second-placed Alfa 33/3 of Toine Hezemans/Masten Gregory without too much bother, and then set off after the leader – the Porsche 908/2 of Peter Revson. After a

spirited battle with the Porsche, Andretti finally got past to take the flag just 22 seconds ahead of the flying Revson. Sam Posey recalled the moment Andretti left the pits: 'Towards the end, Revson was having a magnificent drive in the Porsche and he and Steve McQueen were doing incredibly well, so it was up to Mario to close the gap and get by them. After the last stop, Andretti left the pits at full racing speed, he just tore out of the pits and it was a miracle that he didn't kill 20 people!'

The race for the #24 Chinetti car (chassis 1006), driven by Sam Posey/Ronnie Bucknum, did not end as well, unfortunately. While Sam Posey was driving, he found that the steering wheel was coming loose: 'We had the most ghastly run,' he recalled. 'I was driving and the steering wheel was coming loose and threatened to come off in my hands, and the clutch was going too, and that isn't what you want at Sebring. So I was shifting without the clutch and holding the wheel in place at the same time in this rather high-performance car. I finished my stint and handed over to Ronnie Bucknum.'

Several sources reported that Bucknum had enjoyed himself at a rather jolly party the night before, the effects of which were evident this day. Posey again: 'He made a terrible mistake, he got a flat tyre, and unfortunately missed the inroad to the pits, which left him 5.2 miles to get back to the pits. He didn't, however, make it nearly that

far, and by the time he reached the hairpin the thrashing tyre had wiped out the radiator, which caused the engine to seize. The car veered off the road and crashed into the guard rail and was nearly totalled. So in effect his flat tyre had turned the 512 into a wreck. Not good.'

In summary, the #21 factory 512 S driven by Giunti/Vaccarella/Andretti (chassis 1026) finished first, and was the only 512 to record a finish. The #19 factory car originally driven by Andretti/Merzario (chassis 1010) and the #20 factory car of Ickx/Schetty (chassis 1012) were both non-finishers, together with the #24 NART/Chinetti 512 S of Posey/Bucknum.

Looking back on the race, Forghieri recalled that, 'The Sebring victory with Mario was my favourite 512 memory.'

Thruxton, RAC Sports Car Championship

(Round 2, non-Championship race) 30 March 1970

The race at the end of March at Thruxton in Hampshire, in the south of England, was indeed a round in the RAC Sports Car Championship, but it didn't count towards the World Championships. Despite its slightly lowly status on the international scene, it nevertheless attracted a Porsche 917, a Porsche 910 (driven by Paul Vesty) and a brace of Lola T70s and Chevron B6s, B8s and B16s. One

ABOVE Mario Andretti joined Ignazio Giunti/ Nino Vaccarella in the #21 works car (chassis 1026) to give Ferrari its first win in the 512 S, in the 1970 Sebring 12-Hours. (LAT)

might therefore ask why drivers of such potent machinery took time out to compete in this event, and the answer may lie in the fact that it offered a good opportunity to compete on a fast circuit without travelling to far-flung arenas around the world. The race was won by Jo Siffert in the Porsche 917.

Brands Hatch 1,000km
12 April 1970

It is indeed an unfortunate state of affairs when two important events are held on the same weekend. This happened when the Brands Hatch 1,000km clashed with the Le Mans test weekend, which saw the top teams having to shuttle their star drivers back and forth across the Channel between the two events. This was disruptive in the extreme, as not only is the focus of the teams split but the drivers can't give of their best either. Needless to say, both events were crucial, the Brands Hatch race being part of the International Championship for Manufacturers, and the Le Mans test weekend being the test and set-up opportunity for teams

and drivers ahead of that great race. The factory teams and their drivers could not afford to miss either.

As can be imagined, certain drivers just couldn't be in the right places at the right times, so Jackie Oliver sat in for Mario Andretti and Chris Amon was partnered with Merzario. Georges Filipinetti entered the #3 Ferrari 512 S (chassis 1016), to be driven by Herbert Müller/ Mike Parkes. In addition to these three cars, chassis 1018 was entered by Georg Loos, but since the team hadn't brought any rain tyres with them – certainly a rather important omission when planning a race in Britain – they were unable to start.

The Brands Hatch race was the first Ferrari/ Porsche contest on British or European soil, which in itself was significant, because the races were within reach of a large Ferrari

BELOW The #2 Chris Amon/Arturo Merzario car (chassis 1012) approaches the very tricky Druids bend at Brands Hatch in 1970. (Mike Hayward)

ABOVE The #1 512 S
of Jacky Ickx/Jackie
Oliver (chassis 1010)
would finish in eighth
place at Brands Hatch.
(Mike Hayward)

support base. It was New Zealander Chris
Amon who set the fastest qualifying time of
1:28.6 in the #2 Ferrari, with the Ickx/Oliver
#1 factory 512 in second place. Three rather
tentative laps behind the safety car ensued
at the start before third-placed Vic Elford, in a
factory 917, grabbed the lead in the spray.

The heavy rain affected everybody differently,
and spins were frequent, but while the Porsches
coped adequately Ickx's Ferrari had wiper
problems and had to be reset. Ferrari's pit work
wasn't a match for the clinical efficiency of the
Porsche garages, and unnecessary time was
lost. Matters got worse for Ferrari when the #1
factory Ferrari of Jackie Oliver (chassis 1010)
collided with the #3 Filipinetti Ferrari (chassis
1016) driven by Herbert Müller. While both cars
continued, neither was at its best. Some fine,
equally-matched racing ensued between the
Ferraris and the Porsches. The first three places
seemed assured for the Porsches, as there
were enough laps separating each car, but a
glorious scrap for fourth place was in progress
between the Porsche 908/2 of Gijs van Lennep/
Hans Laine and the Ferrari of Amon/Merzario.

In the end a faulty gearbox in the Ferrari gave
the advantage to van Lennep and Laine, and
so the top four places went to Porsche, while
the highest-finishing factory Ferrari 512 S, that
of Amon/Merzario, came home fifth. The #1
factory Ferrari driven by Jacky Ickx/Jackie Oliver

OPPOSITE Ignazio
Giunti, Nino Vaccarella
and Chris Amon
finished second in the
Monza 1,000km on 25
April 1970, driving the
#3 works car (chassis
1004). *(LAT)*

(chassis 1010) finished in eighth place and
the #3 Filipinetti car (chassis 1016) of Herbert
Müller/Mike Parkes finished 13th.

Monza 1,000km
25 April 1970

Being Ferrari's home race, the 512s were out in
force, a flock of six cars being made up of three
works cars and three privateers. The works cars
were to be driven by Amon/Merzario, Schetty/
John Surtees and Giunti/Vaccarella, the last
pairing driving a Spider-bodied 512 S. As we
have seen, the difference between the Coupé
and the Spider was that the latter simply had
a panel cut out of the roof. Georges Filipinetti,
Picchio Rosso and Georg Loos made up the
privateer entrants. Porsche went one better,
with four works cars and three privateer entries.

Jo Siffert put the 917 Gulf Porsche on pole
followed a half-second back by the Amon/
Merzario works Ferrari. The first three rows
of the grid were arranged in a convenient
alternating pattern of Porsche-Ferrari-Porsche
back to seventh place, which no doubt thrilled
the crowds. The *Tifosi* got even more excited
when, as the flag fell, Ignazio Giunti shot
between the two cars on the front row of the
grid to take the lead, which he held for the first
four laps. The Ferrari had a 917 right on his tail,
so the train of Ferrari-Porsche cars circulated as
if attached by a single, long chain, until Pedro

Rodríguez's and Jo Siffert's John Wyer-entered 917s slipped by.

Once again the chaotic goings-on in the Ferrari pits seemed to be highlighted by the sheer efficiency of the Porsche pit stops, and in this way valuable seconds were gained by the Gulf cars. Towards the end of the race the lead Porsche was forced into retirement when a blown rear tyre took much of the bodywork with it, gifting the lead to relatively inexperienced Finnish driver Leo Kinnunen. Giunti moved into second place by default and set about passing Kinnunen for the lead, which he achieved without too much bother. A late stop for the Ferrari for fuel was nothing short of shambolic, the refuelling process being so badly carried out that Giunti lost his lead to the clockwork-like Porsche pit stop. Rodríguez headed out of the pits in the lead and was never headed.

Although the win went to Porsche, the three Ferrari 512 S factory cars finished in second (chassis 1004), third (chassis 1042) and fourth (chassis 1026) places. The Filipinetti car (chassis 1016) finished in eighth place, while one place back was the Manfredini-entered 512 S (chassis 1022). The spectacle of the Ferrari/Porsche battle was no doubt enjoyed immensely by the crowds – being, of course, what they had paid to see.

Targa Florio
3 May 1970

The Ferrari 512 S is about as well suited to the Sicilian event as a greyhound is to an ice rink. There was no doubting the car's speed, but there was a good reason why Porsche didn't send their all-conquering 917s to compete: the twisty, mountainous circuit demanded the nimble footwork and pinpoint wheel positioning of a ballet dancer.

Needless to say, Ferrari sent a car for local hero Nino Vaccarella and Ignazio Giunti (chassis 1004) to drive, while the Filipinetti team provided a car for Herbert Müller and Mike Parkes (chassis 1016). Against all expectations the Ferraris gave a good account of themselves, but the bumpy circuit gave the Ferrari drivers blisters that slowed them considerably in the closing stages. The more agile Porsche 908s were better suited to the circuit, finishing first and second, but the works Ferrari finished in third place with the Filipinetti car in sixth.

ABOVE In the #22
works car (chassis
1026), Ignazio Giunti/
Nino Vaccarella
finished in fourth
place in the Spa-
Francorchamps
1,000km on 17 May
1970, three laps behind
the winner. (LAT)

Spa-Francorchamps 1,000km
17 May 1970

The third European event of the season would see some of the fastest, most spectacular and closest racing ever. The Porsche 917s were now fitted with the larger 4.9-litre engines, while the Ferraris had had some kinks ironed out. The six Porsche 917s were countered by four Ferrari 512s, of which three were works cars. Porsche driver Pedro Rodríguez set the blindingly quick time of 3:19.8 in the 917, a full 11 seconds quicker than the existing Formula 1 record at the circuit. The quality of the drivers included undoubtedly the finest in the world, with the likes of Rodríguez, Siffert, Brian

Redman, Ickx, Bell, Elford and others setting the circuit alight.

Rodríguez was on pole in the John Wyer Porsche, with the Siffert/Redman Porsche in second place and the Ferrari 512 S of Ickx/ Surtees in third. The top three, Rodríguez, Siffert and local boy Ickx, tore away from the start and the trio ran abreast up the Masta Straight, but as the Ferrari didn't have the top speed of the Porsches it dropped back slightly but remained in close contact with the leaders. Ickx was able to take the lead in the #20 Ferrari (chassis 1038) when Rodríguez pitted to have a tyre replaced. Ickx handed over to Surtees at the change and Redman took over from Siffert.

RIGHT Showing great
potential at Spa in
1970 were Derek Bell/
Hughes de Fierlant
in the distinctive #23
Jacques Swaters
512 S (chassis 1030).
It was Bell's first drive
in a sports car, and he
finished eighth. (LAT)

At the second changeover Surtees stayed behind the wheel, while Siffert took over from Redman and Rodríguez had to give the wheel to Kinnunen. Both Redman and Siffert were quicker than Surtees, so the Porsche led the race while Surtees held station in second. When Kinnunen's gearbox failed the Porsche of Elford/Ahrens stepped up to third spot, which meant the finishing order was Siffert/Redman, Ickx/Surtees and Elford/Ahrens. The top eight places were equally split between Porsche 917s and Ferrari 512s, but Porsche had taken the laurels once again.

Nürburgring 1,000km
31 May 1970

With the positive Targa Florio results still fresh in their minds, Ferrari sent a trio of 512s to the Eifel Mountains to compete against the Porsche 908s. The German cars were once again better suited to the circuit, which consisted of 44 laps of the twisty, undulating 14-mile course. Supporting the works Ferraris was a single Filipinetti entry, to be driven again by Herbert Müller and Mike Parkes (chassis 1008). The three works cars were to be driven by Surtees/Vaccarella (chassis 1042), Giunti/Merzario (chassis 1010) and Ickx/Schetty (chassis 1012), though the last was destroyed in a pre-race accident.

Ferrari's fortunes waxed and waned throughout the race, and although the 908s once again took first and second places the quality driving of Surtees ensured a fine third

place for Maranello. The Filipinetti car finished just one place further back in fourth.

Le Mans 24-Hours
13/14 June 1970

There were no fewer than 11 Ferrari 512s in the field for the 24-Hours of Le Mans in 1970. Four of these were entered by the factory (Ickx/Schetty, Vaccarella/Giunti, Bell/Ronnie Peterson and Merzario/Clay Regazzoni), three were entered by Georges Filipinetti (Manfredini/Moretti, Müller/Parkes and Joakim Bonnier/Reine Wisell), two were entered by Luigi Chinetti (Posey/Bucknum and Helmut Kellerners/Georg Loos), and one each by Escuderia Montjuich and Jacques Swater's Ecurie Francorchamps, driven by José Juncadella/Juan Fernandez and Hughes de Fierlant/Alistair Walker respectively. Ferrari seemed to be taking a leaf out of Porsche's book, at least insofar as there was safety in numbers, as they were up against no fewer than seven Porsche 917s; but even a trusty old Porsche 908/2 would feature in the top three. All four of the Ferrari factory cars as well as two of the privateer 512s were fitted with long tails.

Qualifying would see Porsche 917s in first and third places, split by the factory Ferrari 512 S of Nino Vaccarella/Ignazio Giunti. The race start was a bit of a hybrid affair in that the traditional sprint across the track had been banned, but in an effort to retain some of the old Le Mans style the cars were lined up diagonally against the pit wall, but with the

drivers seated and buckled in. As the clock struck 4:00pm the starter's flag fell and the drivers coaxed their steeds into life, with the 917s of Elford and Siffert being the first two away. It wasn't long before a conrod punched a hole through the engine wall of the #6 works Ferrari of Vaccarella/Giunti (chassis 1026), ending their race after just seven laps.

In the early evening, with light rain falling, the #14 Ferrari driven by Reine Wisell (chassis 1008), whose windscreen was oil smeared, was set upon by three other Ferraris. First on the scene was Derek Bell (chassis 1026), who managed to swerve and miss the struggling Wisell, but this rendered the car unseen by Regazzoni (chassis 1034) and Parkes (chassis 1016) who were close behind Bell. In the ensuing impact, the Ferraris of Wisell, Regazzoni and Parkes were destroyed beyond repair, while Bell limped around for just half a lap more before his car came to a stop, the result of engine damage. This brought the total of Ferrari 512 retirees to five, with barely 40 laps on the board.

Derek Bell recalled the incident: 'I was doing my second stint, and I was coming out of Arnage with a group of cars behind me. Going through the cutting down to Maison Blanche, I came up behind the Ferrari of Reine Wisell going slowly down the middle of the road, and of course I had my foot down because they were right up behind me. I could only squeeze past between the guard rail and the car with two wheels on the dirt at 170mph, and I looked in my mirrors once I had got straightened up,

and there were just cars flying through the air. Clay Regazzoni was on the guard rail and flames were pouring from his Ferrari but I was well past them by now. I went past the pits and got on to the Mulsanne Straight again but then the engine blew up. And so I eventually got a ride back to the pits in a car and when I got back the team manager came up to me and asked if I was all right, and of course I replied "Yes." But he said, "You were in that crash." Then I told him that the car was out, parked on the Mulsanne Straight, but they didn't know that because there wasn't the TV coverage in those days. So that was me out of Le Mans, and the end of the 512.'

Dick Fritz was very complimentary about Sam Posey as a driver. Posey recalled an incident during the 1970 Le Mans with a smile. 'He said that only because I kept my mouth shut about something that happened during the race! I was going along, following a car whose engine blew right in front of me, and it covered the windshield with oil. I stopped at the pits, barely able to see, and I sat there waiting for them to clean the windscreen but nobody arrived to attend to the car. Not seeing anybody around, I got out, climbed over the pit wall and found all the mechanics asleep, so I thought, why wake them up? And I cleaned the windshield myself and got back in and drove on.'

The 1970 race will be remembered as one of the wettest in many years, and the rate of attrition was staggering, with only 15 cars being classified at the end of the race. Only two of the Ferrari 512s finished the race: the Chinetti car driven by Sam Posey/Ronnie Bucknum (chassis

LEFT Finishing in fifth place at Le Mans that year, one position behind the Chinetti car but eight laps adrift, were Hughes de Fierlant/Alistair Walker in the #12 Jacques Swaters 512 S (chassis 1030). *(LAT)*

BELOW Four-into-one won't go, as the two lead 917s and two 512s jostle for that ideal position on the apex of the first corner at the start of the Watkins Glen 6-Hours on 11 July 1970. Eventually it was the #92 works car of Mario Andretti/Ignazio Giunti (chassis 1042) that finished third, with the #91 factory car of Jacky Ickx/Peter Schetty (chassis 1010) in fifth place. *(LAT)*

1014), and the Jacques Swaters-entered car of Hughes de Fierlant/Alistair Walker (chassis 1030), which finished fifth. 'We finished fourth, which sounds pretty good,' said Posey, 'but we were the first of the Ferraris, which sounds even better. Then I looked at the results, and I realised that there were only eight cars still running at the end, so instead of finishing a glorious fourth we finished midfield if you look at it that way! But we were very proud – we beat all the factory Ferraris, of which a few went out due to driver error in the rain. Although we took it easily, it was still very difficult going.'

Watkins Glen 6-Hours
11 July 1970

Although Porsche had already taken the World Championship after their win at Le Mans, they still made a strong appearance at Watkins Glen. Ferrari, though, only put forward two factory cars, one for Ickx/Schetty (chassis 1010) and the other for American hero Mario Andretti and Ignazio Giunti (chassis 1042). One private 512 S, entered by Georg Loos, was driven by Loos and Franz Pesch (chassis 1018). The two works Ferraris were open-top Spider versions.

Although Siffert was on pole with a John Wyer

ABOVE Jacky Ickx and Peter Schetty finished fifth at the 1970 Watkins Glen 6-Hours in the #91 works car (chassis 1010). *(LAT)*

Porsche 917, it was Andretti who made the best of the rolling start, squeezing Siffert against the inside kerb in the first corner. The Watkins Glen circuit had just been resurfaced, and this made it quite difficult and slippery, forcing the cars to drive on intermediate tyres. Siffert quickly made good his early misdemeanour and slipped ahead of the Ferrari, with Rodríguez, in the second Wyer Porsche, in pursuit. While Siffert and Rodríguez went hammer and tongs at each other, Andretti was fighting his own battle with intermittent fuel pump problems.

In the end the two Wyer Porsches proved too quick for the opposition, and comfortably took first and second place, while Andretti brought the Ferrari home in third.

Österreichring 1,000km
11 October 1970

In the last Championship race of the season, all the top teams wanted to end the season on a high, although Ferrari hoped to do so with just one works entry. Jacky Ickx and Ignazio Giunti (chassis 1010) would represent the Italian marque along with the privately entered Georg Loos 512 S, which he again shared with Franz Pesch.

Although Rodríguez had pole position from Ickx by three-tenths of a second, it was Ickx who was first away. His car, sporting a slightly longer tail that hinted at the 512 M for the 1971 season, ran well at the front for a while until electrical problems halted the car out on the circuit. After returning to the pits the car did make it back into the fray but it soon retired, ending a very disappointing year for the factory.

Kyalami 9-Hours
(Non-Championship race)
7 November 1970

In warm conditions and under sunny skies, Ferrari at last beat their rivals from Stuttgart in a comprehensive manner. Jacky Ickx, partnered with Ignazio Giunti, put the works Ferrari 512 M (chassis 1010) on pole with a time of 1:22.400, while Derek Bell and Hughes de Fierlant in the Jacques Swaters Ecurie Francorchamps 512 S (chassis 1030) were placed three positions further back.

Ickx started the race and immediately took

RIGHT The cover of the 1970 Kyalami 9-Hour race programme showed the two top contenders, a Porsche 917 and a Ferrari 512 S. *(Virtual Motorpix)*

the lead, having little trouble in staying well ahead of the 917s – which was most uncharacteristic, when looking back over the season – and that's the way it stayed, with Ickx/Giunti finishing first having completed 370 laps and the Bell/de Fierlant car back in sixth place on 346 laps.

Ironically, it was now – just when it seemed that the 512 M had achieved its required levels of performance and reliability – that Ferrari dropped all further development of the car and handed the running of their sports cars over to private race teams. In the words of János Wimpffen in his book *Time and Two Seats*, 'Throughout the maiden year of the 512 S, they showed either speed, reliability, good strategy, or luck. But they were never able to demonstrate any two of these traits at the same time.' It had also become obvious to many that Ferrari was spreading itself too thinly, by trying to compete at the highest possible level in too many different classes of motor sport. Wimpffen summed it up well when he stated, 'Ferrari was defeated by both Porsche and themselves.'

Racing in 1971

With Ferrari having withdrawn its official factory participation in sports car racing, no further development of the 512 took place in 1971. This was in order to focus resources on their Formula 1 programme and the new 3-litre 312 PB model. However, fortunately for the

BELOW Daytona 1971 featured three top players: the #6 Sunoco Penske 512 M (chassis 1040, finished third) leads the #2 Porsche (eventual winner) and the #23 Chinetti Ferrari 512 S that finished second (chassis 1006). *(LAT)*

privateer teams Mauro Forghieri had carried out some much-needed development on the 512 at the back end of 1970, and as a result the 1971 512 M was a much more refined racer.

Despite this being the final year for the 5-litre Group 5 cars, the interest insofar as the public was concerned lay in these blisteringly fast and hugely impressive machines. While Ferrari chose to halt development of their 512 sports car, Porsche by contrast chose to invest even more resources in their 917 model for racing beyond the end of the season in the all-important Can-Am series.

Always looking for a steed with which to compete in a popular series, Penske sought out a 512 S to convert to M-spec and to prepare for the 1971 season. In late 1970, he approached a man who had his ear close to the ground in the world of 'used' Ferrari race cars, Kirk White, and suggested that they form a consortium to buy and race a 512 the next season. The story of the development of the Penske/White Sunoco 512 M is covered in Chapter 4, but suffice it to say that the race car that rolled off the Penske transporter at the first race of the season caused many a seasoned race goer to take a sharp intake of breath. In short, it was stunning and fast!

Buenos Aires 1,000km
10 January 1971

Although not a big event, this was the first round of the Manufacturers' Championship and it served as an important shakedown race for the rest of the season. The quality of the driver line-up reflected its importance. John Wyer had his two works 917 K racers in a field of seven 917s, while four Ferrari 512s added further weight to the grid. The Ferraris were a mixed lot, with one each for Chinetti to be driven by Sam Posey/Nestor Garcia-Veiga/Rubén Luis di Palma (512 S chassis 1006); the Filipinetti car was driven by Mike Parkes/Jo Bonnier (512 M chassis 1048); the Jacques Swaters car was driven by Hughes de Fierlant/Gustave Gosselin (512 S chassis 1030); and the Juncadella car was driven by José Juncadella himself and Carlos Pairetti (512 S chassis 1002).

Unfortunately, during the race Ignazio Giunti – in a Ferrari 312 PB – collided with the almost stationary Matra of Jean-Pierre Beltoise,

causing a huge accident that resulted in Giunti's death. The race was red-flagged while the resultant mess was cleared up, but the restart was chaotic in that when it was announced that the race would resume some drivers began racing without reforming on the grid. The authorities eventually let the racing continue, but sadly the Ferraris just weren't on the pace as two Alfa Romeo 33/3s separated them from the two John Wyer Porsches.

The Wyer cars took first and second places, with the four Ferrari 512s taking fifth through eighth. The top-finishing Ferrari was the #20 Juncadella car, followed by the #18 car entered by Jacques Swaters in sixth, the #8 Filipinetti car in seventh and the #22 Chinetti Ferrari in eighth.

Daytona 24-Hours
30/31 January 1971

Apart from the John Wyer Porsches no other manufacturers were officially present at the 1971 Daytona 24-Hours, at least not directly, and this was due in part to the global economic downturn. Also playing into this uncertain landscape was the 3-litre engine capacity limit planned for the 1972 season, which was looming on the horizon.

On the grid was an armada of no fewer than six Ferrari 512s, equally split between the older S version and the new M version. Lining up alongside them on the entry list was a squad of four 917s, while the only other realistic contender on paper was the Chinetti-entered Ferrari 312 P. Mark Donohue put the immaculately turned out Roger Penske-entered #6 Sunoco 512 M on pole with a time of 1:42.42, with the #2 Porsche 917 second and the #22 Chinetti-entered Ferrari 512 M of Peter Revson and Sam Posey in third.

The Penske Ferrari was originally a 1970 512 S Spider, but for 1971 had been modified into a 512 M Coupé for Mark Donohue and David Hobbs. These formed a formidable team in the Sunoco-sponsored car, which boasted a 640bhp Traco-prepared engine. In fact, the pole time set by Donohue shattered the previous lap record of 1:51.6 set by Mario Andretti the year before in a works Ferrari 512 S. To be fair, much of the more than nine-second time differential could be attributed to a resurfaced infield section, but there was no denying the level of

preparation that Penske had gone to with the Sunoco Ferrari.

NART driver Sam Posey remembered: 'That was an important race to me because Mr Chinetti let me have the driver of my choice, and so I signed Peter Revson. I was very anxious at that point to see how I stacked up against him, and I actually faired all right. I was faster in the night and he was faster in the day, but there was only a couple of tenths in it.'

But as so often happens in these long endurance races, general wear and tear and plain old circumstances play a big hand in the outcome, and the 1971 Daytona was no exception. While Donohue/Hobbs experienced electrical problems early on, they recovered to remain within sight of the leaders until the Ferrari became inadvertently involved in an accident during the small hours. The accident was the result of Vic Elford slamming into the wall on the banking when a tyre blew on his Porsche 917, and as Donohue tiptoed through the debris he was in turn hit by a 911 which then also hit Elford's car. Fortunately, no one was seriously hurt in the ensuing chaos. The

repairs to the Donohue/Hobbs car took an hour and ten minutes and included significant work on the body as well as the car's suspension. The Chinetti boys stepped in with some replacement suspension parts that Penske didn't have to hand. The previously beautifully prepared dark blue Sunoco Ferrari now looked like it had spent the night in the emergency department of the local hospital, bandaged end to end in silver duct tape.

Woody Woodard, the Penske chief mechanic, outlined the suspension repair: 'At Daytona we sat on pole, being significantly quicker than the 917 Ks. At around midnight we were leading the race by several laps when there was a shunt which was started by Elford, who lost control of his 917, and then a 911 ran into us. Anyway, Mark limped back into the pits with the entire left front corner of the car removed – no suspension, no nothing, all gone! I threw in the towel, but Roger said, "No, we're going to try." And so I started to pull the thing apart, and one of the mechanics went out into the parking lot and found another 512 that had blown its engine, and we literally borrowed

the parts off this other car in the middle of the night. So we got the suspension back together and set the toe-in, but the biggest problem was that although we had a spare nose, there was no support on the left front corner to hold the nose on. I wound up rigging an array of broomsticks with about 30 rolls of silver tape to hold everything together, and after about two hours we got the car back together. When Mark went back out I think we were 11 laps behind and he made up all but three of those laps and finished third. I mean, the car was quick, it looked gorgeous, but we didn't win the race.'

Dick Fritz, the Chinetti team manager, also recalled the incident with some humour. 'I do remember Daytona 1971. It was said that Roger had got the 512 and redesigned everything – the suspension was different, and the engine, which was built by Traco, developed around 600bhp. When the Penske car crashed, they were pitted just before us in the pit lane, and so the car came in and we saw the left front suspension had been all smashed in. Roger came over to me and said, "Do you by any chance have a suspension all assembled and everything that I could have?" I said, "Yes, but it won't do you

any good because your car is all different." And he said, "My car isn't different, it's the same damn car," so I said, "OK, you can have it."'

The #20 Chinetti-entered Ferrari 512 M of Masten Gregory/Gregg Young was out after just 16 laps with a thrown conrod. The other Chinetti Ferrari 512 M, driven by Revson/Posey, blew its engine after 202 laps. The third Chinetti-entered Ferrari, the #23 512 S of Ronnie Bucknum/Tony Adamowicz, experienced electrical problems, but a marathon 90-minute gearbox rebuild to the leading Porsche of Pedro Rodríguez/ Jackie Oliver in the 22nd hour enabled the Ferrari to turn a 209-mile deficit into a two-lap lead with just 45 minutes to go. But then it was the turn of the Ferrari to succumb to soft valve springs, which sapped the car's power and cost Bucknum/Adamowicz an extra ten seconds per lap. This was just enough to let the resurgent Porsche catch and overtake the struggling Ferrari, resulting in the tightest finish at Daytona in the race's ten-year history.

Dick Fritz shared his memory of this incident: 'We had Ronnie Bucknum driving with Tony Adamowicz and we almost won that race. We lost by half a lap after 24 hours. A valve had got bent in our engine so it was running pretty much on 11 cylinders, and then Pedro Rodríguez came in with a broken gearbox. They were pitted about two or three pits before us, and I went over and watched them putting the gearbox together. Pedro had been well ahead of us until finally, after the gearbox broke, we took the lead, and I said to Pedro, "Pedro, I would really like to win this race, you're not going to go out and try and beat us are you?" He said with a smile, "Well, you know that is my job." So he went out and he caught up to us for sure with a healthy car, but we almost won.'

The Rodríguez/Oliver Porsche was followed home by the #23 Bucknum/Adamowicz Ferrari, with the heavily bandaged #6 Sunoco Ferrari of Donohue/Hobbs in third place. The determined drive by Bucknum/Adamowicz earned them the 'True Grit' award for converting a 200-plus mile shortfall into a two-lap lead with less than two hours remaining. Donohue did have the satisfaction of setting a fastest race lap of 1:41.25, remarkably more than a second quicker than his pole-setting time.

Sebring 12-Hours
20 March 1971

Despite its Daytona bashing, the Penske Sunoco car was repaired in time for Sebring, where this time the drama started before the car had even reached the circuit when Donohue twisted his ankle loading the Ferrari at the workshop. Donohue then had to drive the transporter to Sebring himself. As Penske didn't know how bad Donohue's ankle was he had to get his own racing licence reinstated after a six-year lapse, just in case he had to partner David Hobbs as co-driver. Fortunately, Donohue was pronounced fit at his medical and Penske didn't have to drive. (See boxout overleaf.)

ABOVE The #28 José Juncadella-entered Ferrari 512 S driven by Arturo Merzario/José Juncadella (chassis 1002) retired after 161 laps with fuel pump problems. *(LAT)*

GETTING TO SEBRING

Penske's Woody Woodard recalled the lead up to the Sebring race: 'We'd been pulling 24-hour days getting the car ready for Sebring. We were loading up the car the night before we had to get there, and Mark said, "You guys go home and rest up before you get on a plane in the morning, and I'll drive the truck down to the circuit." Then in the process of loading the car he sprained his ankle, but that was after I'd already gone home. So, not knowing anything about it, we flew down to Sebring the next morning on Roger's Lear jet.

'Back then, the check-in for the Sebring race and technical inspection was done in the downtown square in Sebring town. So we were there waiting for the car when Roger got a call from Mark saying that he'd been an hour and a half away when the engine failed on the transporter, but he'd arranged to have a big tow truck pick it up and tow it the rest of the way. So we waited there on pins and needles, and when it finally showed up it was late afternoon, perhaps about four o'clock. Mark was still

in severe pain from his sprained ankle, so Roger sent him to the hotel to rest up and told him that we would have Hobbs drive night practice that night, so Mark wasn't even going to get into the car until the next day.

'We pulled the car out of the transporter, then the transporter left for the racetrack and we pushed the car to technical inspection. The scrutineers just walked around it a couple of times – I didn't even lift the engine cover, and they passed it! Roger then said he'd drive the car to the racetrack and set off through the orange groves. I remember it was just a two-lane back road, but we had to cross some train tracks and I was concerned about bottoming out the nose, so I got out and walked alongside the car. He had to approach the railway tracks at an angle so he didn't bottom out, but we eventually got to the racetrack in time. The guys had in the meantime unloaded the pit equipment and Hobbs drove the car for the night practice, but Mark was fine for the race the next day and he put it on pole.'

BELOW Despite being rear-ended by Rodríguez in the Porsche, Donohue brought the #6 Penske Sunoco Ferrari (chassis 1040) home in fourth place in the 1971 Daytona 24-Hours. (LAT)

In true style, Donohue (chassis 1040) set the fastest qualifying time, with Revson seventh in the #22 Chinetti 512 M (chassis 1020), Masten Gregory eighth in the Irene Young-entered 512 M (chassis 1014) and Ronnie Bucknum ninth in the #23 Chinetti 512 S (chassis 1006). Chinetti's third 512 (chassis 1028), driven by Chuck Parsons/David Weir, was gridded in 12th place.

The speed differential between the fastest and slowest cars was significant, but the quickest drivers required only that the slowest cars didn't make any allowances when being overtaken. This allowed the faster drivers to know where the slower cars would be on the track and when taking lines through corners, so that overtaking moves could be carried out with more assurance.

The Penske car took an early lead at the start of the race and held it for the first 20 laps, while Andretti in a Ferrari 312 PB battled with the Porsches a little way back. When Revson came in for his first fuel stop the car wouldn't restart – the crew tried jumper cables and a new battery, but nothing seemed to help the stricken Ferrari. The electrical master switch was eventually replaced, but tracing the problem had cost the team 48 minutes.

The other Chinetti car didn't fare much better when the throttle on the Parsons 512 S jammed open, causing him to ram into a sandbank. He managed to get the car back to the pits, but the impact had damaged the car's suspension and it was forced to retire after just 20 laps. A spectacular accident occurred a short while later when the brakes on Gregg Young's car failed and he slammed into the same sandbank that Parsons had attacked. This time the Ferrari's momentum carried it right up the bank, whereupon it launched into the air before flipping and twisting in mid-air, crashing to the ground and bursting into flames. Fortunately, Young was pulled free after the three corner marshals levered the car up under very dangerous conditions, a selfless act that earned them the Hayden Williams Sportsmanship Award.

Next, following a pit stop to replace a torn tyre, Donohue came up to lap Rodríguez, who was doing what any driver would do which was to make his car as wide as possible. Donohue spotted his chance when Rodríguez was stuck behind a slower car, allowing the Ferrari to slip by. But as the Ferrari overtook the Porsche, Rodríguez turned out too soon and the front right of his car crunched into the left rear of the Ferrari. They both limped back to the pits, where the Ferrari lost 21 laps undergoing

BELOW Driving the #22 Chinetti 512 M (chassis 1020), Peter Revson and Swede Savage retired after 169 laps of the 1971 Daytona race – more than half-distance – due to gearbox problems. *(LAT)*

ABOVE Both of these Ferraris retired early from the 1971 Sebring 12-Hours: the #20 Irene Young-entered 512 M driven by Masten Gregory/ Gregg Young (chassis 1014) succumbed to an accident after just 29 laps; and the #23 Chinetti 512 S of Ronnie Bucknum/Sam Posey (chassis 1006) lost oil pressure after 114 laps. (LAT)

repairs while the Porsche sustained only a flat tyre and front wing damage.

'Mark was significantly quicker than Rodríguez,' Woody Woodard commented, 'but the two of them got into a fisticuffs when Pedro rammed into the left rear and blew our left rear tyre. The tyre shredded and came apart, ripping up the left rear fuel bladder, which we then had to repair. We rigged something up to continue in the race, but we had very slow fuel stops because we couldn't vent the bladder properly.'

The two remaining Chinetti Ferraris, those of Ronnie Bucknum/Sam Posey (chassis 1006) and Peter Revson/Swede Savage (chassis 1020), also retired, the former with oil pressure problems after 114 laps and the latter as a result of a gearbox failure after 169 laps. The only Ferrari 512 to finish was the rather battered-looking Penske car, which finished in sixth place.

Brands Hatch 1,000km
4 April 1971

The first of the European rounds of the World Championship saw just two Ferrari 512 Ms up against five Porsche 917s, but the opposition this time would come from the new Group 6 cars. Brands Hatch favoured the nimbler Ferrari 312 PBs and the Alfa Romeo 33/3s, and they didn't disappoint.

The highest Ferrari 512 qualifier was the Juncadella-entered car (chassis 1002) driven by David Hobbs/José Juncadella, in eighth place, with the Herbert Müller-entered car driven by himself and René Herzog (chassis 1044) in 11th. Both Ferrari 512s were originally S-spec cars converted to M-spec for the 1971 season.

On pole was the 312 of Ickx/Regazzoni, with the Alfa of Ralf Stommelen/Toine Hezemans second followed by the Porsche 917 of Siffert/ Bell. The start was a wet affair, with most cars

LEFT Finishing in fifth
place at Brands Hatch
on 4 April 1971 was
the #3 Ferrari 512 M
(chassis 1002) driven
by David Hobbs and
José Juncadella.
(Mike Hayward)

ABOVE Entered by Herbert Müller, the #1 Ferrari 512 M (chassis 1044) finished in fourth place at Brands Hatch in 1971, with René Herzog partnering Müller. *(Mike Hayward)*

on wet tyres except for the second-placed Alfa, and no small amount of fancy footwork was required by many of the front runners who had to tiptoe past the struggling Alfa.

While the big players battled it out around the twisty, undulating circuit, the two Ferrari 512s delivered a rather mediocre performance. Finishing in fourth place was the #1 Herbert Müller Ferrari 512 M, with the #3 Ferrari 512 M of Hobbs/Juncadella one place further back.

Monza 1,000km
25 April 1971

The Monza race was never going to be ordinary, as the Italians had come to see their favourite drivers and cars performing in front of a very lively home crowd. The *Tifosi* and the *Alfisti* had come in support of their beloved Ferrari and Alfa Romeo race cars, and they expected results; no other marques really mattered.

Compared with Brands Hatch, where the Group 6 cars had an advantage, Monza was a very different circuit in that it favoured the older Group 5 cars. Having said that, the Group 6 cars now had several races behind them and offered a much-improved performance. The Alfa Romeo in particular had been putting in extremely encouraging performances, but pole position went to the Porsche 917 K of Vic Elford and Gérard Larrousse. Second place was held by

Jacky Ickx/Clay Regazzoni in the Ferrari 312 PB while the Alfa Romeo of Stommelen/Hezemans was in third, which gave the fans something to cheer about. The race's five Ferrari 512s were exceeded in number only by six Porsche 917s, although the Ferraris did comprise a slightly mixed bunch of S- and M-spec cars.

Most people were totally surprised when Mike Parkes took the lead in the very early stages, but the jubilation was not to last as he was quickly swamped by the Porsches and Group 6 Ferraris. Arturo Merzario's 512 (chassis 1002) made contact with a Porsche 907 on the 11th lap, and the two spinning cars took out another three between them, effectively eliminating five cars in one hit.

Merzario's Ferrari was soon joined by the #9 Filipinetti car driven by Corrado Manfredini/Giancarlo Gagliardi (chassis 1050), when it retired after 27 laps with a faulty fuel pump. The #8 Filipinetti car driven by Mike Parkes/Jo Bonnier (chassis 1022), which had led momentarily near the beginning, blew its engine on lap 30 and recorded a DNF. This meant that three of the five 512s that had started the race were out of the running after 30 laps, leaving just the two Müller-entered cars (chassis 1044 and 1008) in contention.

In the closing stages it was the two John Wyer Porsches that literally ran away with the

event. As a consolation for their loyalty the *Alfisti* saw three Alfa Romeos occupy the next three places, with the two remaining Ferrari 512s coming home sixth and eighth.

Spa-Francorchamps 1,000km
9 May 1971
Held under the auspices of the Royal Automobile Club Belgium, the Spa had been run as a 1,000km event since 1966. It was, however, still run over the same 15km (9.3-mile) circuit using the public roads between the towns of Francorchamps, Malmedy and Stavelot that had been used since the first 24-hour race was held there in 1924. Although the Formula 1 contingent deemed it too dangerous for racing the sports car fraternity had no such concerns, and in fact relished the prospect of the high speeds that could be attained there. The 7km circuit used today was inaugurated in 1979.

What the 1971 starting grid may have lacked in quantity, it certainly made up for in quality. The winner was undoubtedly expected to emerge from the ranks of the six Porsche 917s present, as Alfa Romeo had sent just a single car, choosing instead to prepare for the forthcoming Targa Florio to which the nimble Alfa was far better suited. Three Ferrari 512s were also present in the line-up, but they were not thought to pose much of a challenge to the Porsches. This was the last time that the Group 5 racers would race at the Spa circuit, so the Porsche factory cars were like greyhounds waiting for the gates to open and for the hare to be let loose.

As expected, the John Wyer Porsche 917 set the fastest qualifying time, but on this occasion in the hands of young Briton Derek Bell, with the Martini Porsche 917 of Vic Elford in second place. The highest-placed Ferrari 512 was the Filipinetti-entered 512 M (chassis 1050) in sixth place and driven by Gagliardi/Manfredini. The other Ferraris were the Herbert Müller-entered 512 Ms of Müller/René Herzog (chassis 1044) in eighth place and Cox Kocher/Heinrich Wiesendanger (chassis 1016) in tenth.

Siffert and Rodríguez in the two John Wyer Porsches tore away from the start and after the first lap had opened up a 23-second lead on the entire field. Away from the spectacular scrap that was going on at the front, the Ferrari 512 of Müller/Herzog became embroiled in a lengthy tussle with the 917 of Willy Kauhsen, but with 50 laps on the board the Ferrari retired with a blown engine. Out of the running at the start was the second Müller Ferrari of Kocher/Wiesendanger, which stripped the threads on a wheel nut while still on the starting grid and didn't complete a single lap. The third 512 in

ABOVE **The #11 Ferrari 512 M entered by Herbert Müller and driven by Gianpiero Moretti/Teodoro Zeccoli (chassis 1008) enters the pit lane at Monza on 25 April 1971. The car would finish in eighth place overall.** *(LAT)*

the field driven by Gagliardi/Manfredini lasted only one lap more than the Müller/Herzog car, as it too blew its engine on lap 51.

It remains to be said that the Porsches of Siffert/Bell and Rodríguez/Oliver traded the lead throughout the race. Siffert bettered Bell's qualifying time of 3:16.0 with a fastest race lap of 3:14.6, and this race remains the all-time fastest road course race ever, with the 1,000km being completed in just 4 hours 1 minute 9.7 seconds. The winner was the Rodríguez/Oliver Porsche 917, followed by Siffert/Bell in the sister car. There wasn't a Ferrari to be seen anywhere, with even the 312 PB of Ickx/Regazzoni being damaged and not completing the race, so it was not the Maranello brand's finest day.

Nürburgring 1,000km
30 May 1971

Lacking development, and outpaced by most of its immediate competitors, it appeared that the 512s were reduced to also-rans. Once again, three 512s were lined up for the start of the Nürburgring 1,000km, with Herbert Müller entering two cars and the third being that of Georg Loos. The Müller cars were to be driven by the familiar pairings of the car's owner and

René Herzog (chassis 1044) and Cox Kocher/ Heinrich Wiesendanger (chassis 1016). The Loos Ferrari was piloted by its owner and Franz Pesch (chassis 1018).

The Loos Ferrari was the only 512 to finish the race, being placed ninth overall.

Le Mans 24-Hours
12/13 June 1971

The 1971 Le Mans 24-Hours was an important race for a couple of reasons. Firstly because it was the first rolling start at this legendary race and secondly because it was the final time that the Group 5 cars would race the French circuit in anger. Ironically, the Group 6 cars that were to replace them, namely the new generation Ferrari 312 P and the Alfa Romeo 33/3, were notable by their absence.

Nine of the 25 Ferrari 512s produced were on the starting grid for the 1971 Le Mans 24-Hours. This was a really impressive turnout by the privateer teams, which enjoyed no support of any kind from the factory. A Ferrari factory contingent did attend the race, though, perhaps being pushed into making an appearance by the large 512 presence. The nine 512s on the entry list were:

BELOW The #16 Ferrari 512 M (chassis 1028) entered for the 1971 Le Mans race by David Piper and ably driven to a fine fourth-place finish by Chris Craft/David Weir. *(LAT)*

Chassis	Car no	Drivers	Entered by	Grid position
1002	15	Nino Vaccarella/José Juncadella	José Juncadella	6
1006	14	Masten Gregory/George Eaton	NART/Chinetti	15
1018	10	Georg Loos/Franz Pesch	Georg Loos	13
1020	12	Sam Posey/Tony Adamowicz	NART/Chinetti	12
1028	16	Chris Craft/David Weir	David Piper	9
1030	9	Hughes de Fierlant/Alain de Cadenet	Jacques Swaters	10
1032	6	Corrado Manfredini/Giancarlo Gagliardi	Georges Filipinetti	14
1040	11	Mark Donohue/David Hobbs	NART/Chinetti	4
1048	7	Mike Parkes/Henri Pescarolo	Georges Filipinetti	8

Those with a sharp eye will note that the #11 Ferrari of Donohue/Hobbs is listed as being entered in the name of NART/Chinetti. This is not an error, as the car was indeed entered by the NART team for Penske. Dick Fritz, NART/Chinetti team manager, humorously recalled the Penske car being scrutineered: 'I remember standing in the scrutineers' inspection area, which was quite elaborate at Le Mans, and thinking that everybody in the town must have had part of the job of inspecting a car – one fellow at the left rear tail light, another at the signal light...'

Ferrari had come prepared not only with spares for the privateer teams, but had also brought a couple of new engines. The engines were offered to Penske (see below) and to the NART/Chinetti team, as Dick Fritz remembered: 'We didn't have to change our engine because it was running just fine, but the factory rep said that the engines they'd brought from the factory were improved and ready to race, with just dyno time on them. It seemed like a good move to use a fresh engine for the 24 hours rather than one with six or seven hours of track time on it. We changed the engine on the Friday afternoon before the race in the garage that we'd rented in the middle of Le Mans.'

Far from being a spent force, the Penske/Sunoco Ferrari was placed fourth overall in qualifying by Mark Donohue, with a time of 3:18.5. This placed him just behind Rodríguez/

BELOW Entered for the 1971 Le Mans race by José Juncadella and driven by himself and Nino Vaccarella, the #15 Ferrari 512 M (chassis 1002) retired with a broken gearbox, having started from sixth place on the grid. *(LAT)*

Penske chief mechanic Woody Woodard described their engine change the day before the race:

'For Le Mans, we took the old Traco engine in the car and went over there with very limited staff – just myself and my assistant mechanic. Mark had a lot of friends in Europe who could collect the car and get it to Le Mans for us. The car was quick, but it wasn't the fastest, because the two long tail 917s were capable of almost 240mph on the Mulsanne Straight, and the Ferrari was terminal at about 212mph. That was a huge difference, but we were light years ahead of every other Ferrari at the race.

'The factory, who were there to support the privateers, saw how fast we were. They certainly wanted to beat Porsche, and so the day before the race they came to Roger and offered him a brand-new engine that they had at the track in the back of a lorry, because they felt that their engine would have more horsepower than our Traco engine, and they wanted him to put it into the car for the race.

'Roger approached Mark and I, and we talked about it, but in racing I've always said that if you can't test something before the race

starts and you need to make a change, don't make the change. So I said to Roger that we shouldn't change the engine, and Mark tended to agree with me, but Roger always gets three votes to your one, and he said we are going to do it. With that settled, I asked *where* we should do it, so Mark went out and found a gas station that was about two miles from the racetrack, and Mark drove the car there on the highway. I got my toolbox and equipment over there, looked around, and found there was no way to remove the engine – no hoist and no lift. So I said, "Mark, we've no way of getting the engine out," and he told me to get the engine ready and he'd be back.

'About 45 minutes later I heard this very loud diesel-engined vehicle coming up the road, and into the property drove Mark Donohue, driving an absolutely massive four-axle, 16-wheel articulated crane with a ball and hook that weighed more than the car. And he was just grinning from ear to ear, and that is how we changed the engine! A lorry showed up with a new engine, they took the old engine away, and I had to work all night installing the new one. At about seven o'clock the next morning we were finished, and Mark drove it up and down a couple of back roads outside Le Mans just to test everything and to make sure nothing was leaking.

'We started the race, and about four hours into the race we were running second for a while when the engine blew. Our old engine, the Traco that Roger made me take out, was taken away in the lorry by the Ferrari people, and I never saw it again.

'I'd been up for about 36 hours with no sleep, and Mark, after he got out of his driver suit and we knew that our race was done, told us to take his car and go back to the hotel to get some sleep. He said that when we woke up in the morning we were to go to the desk and there might be a message there for us. So we did that, we went back to the hotel, got something to eat and went to sleep. The next morning we went down to the desk at the hotel and there were two first-class Air France tickets back home, with a note from Mark which said that he'd get everything loaded up, and that we should go home!'

BELOW Despite running with a new engine supplied by the factory, the #11 Penske Donohue/ Hobbs car (chassis 1040) failed to deliver at Le Mans in 1971. *(LAT)*

ABOVE Passing the pits in the 1971 Le Mans 24-Hours, the #9 car of Hughes de Fierlant/Alain de Cadenet leads the #12 car of Sam Posey/ Tony Adamowicz. *(LAT)*

Oliver on pole, Elford/Larrousse in second place and Siffert/Bell in third, all driving Porsche 917 LHs. Just behind Donohue/Hobbs was another Porsche 917, that of Helmut Marko/Gijs van Lennep with the Ferrari 512 M of Nino Vaccarella/ José Juncadella one place further back.

Starting from 12th on the grid, Sam Posey set off in the Chinetti Ferrari fully expecting to complete his stint before having to pit again. However this was not to be, as he had to call into the pits after just one lap to report low oil pressure. Fortunately the fault was quickly traced to a malfunctioning gauge, and he was out again before the rest of the field had completed another lap.

Posey picked up the story: 'I pushed it quite hard at the beginning because I had to pit for a gauge that turned out to be malfunctioning, so when I went back out the track was empty because the field was halfway around the lap. So I just went like anything. I slowed down again when I caught up with the others, and it was OK because Mr Chinetti didn't rant and rave. Mr Chinetti was very firm that we weren't to push it too much, but secretly he was pretty excited by it.'

Of the nine 512s that started the 1971 Le Mans 24-Hours only two finished it, with the NART/Chinetti Ferrari of Posey/Adamowicz in third place and the Piper Ferrari of owner David Piper and Chris Craft in fourth place, 11 laps adrift. But it nearly ended in tears for the Posey/ Adamowicz car, as Dick Fritz explained: 'Near

PIT FRACAS

Roger Penske has always played a very active role in his team's activities at the races. Woody Woodard recalled one incident at Le Mans that was quite serious at the time, but in retrospect is fairly humorous:

'Roger has always managed the pits during the race, and he still does so to this day. He's the one who's calling the shots, he's the one who's telling the pit crew what we're going to do. He's the one that tells the driver when to come in, the one that stops the car when it comes into the pits, and the one that tells the driver when to go! And every driver who ever drove a car in a race that he was managing knew that they dared not leave until Roger gave them the sign. So, in the very first pit stop of the race Mark came in for fuel only, but refuelling was slow because it wasn't our quick system – we had to use the French system. Roger was out in front of the car with his hand up, holding it, and Mark was watching him like he always did. When the fueller came out, Roger dropped his hand and Mark took off. Well he *started* to take off, but right behind Roger was an official with a little flag, and – we didn't know it – apparently each pit had a pit official, and only they were supposed to release the car.

'Mark didn't know what to do, because the official was waving his arms and yelling and screaming, and Roger just pushed him out of the way and told Mark to take off. There was a huge flap, officials were running around all over the place, and this guy was absolutely beside himself that he got pushed by Roger. But somehow they came to an agreement in the end because we had the photographer Bernard Cahier assisting us as an interpreter, and I believe he came on the scene and got everything calmed down.'

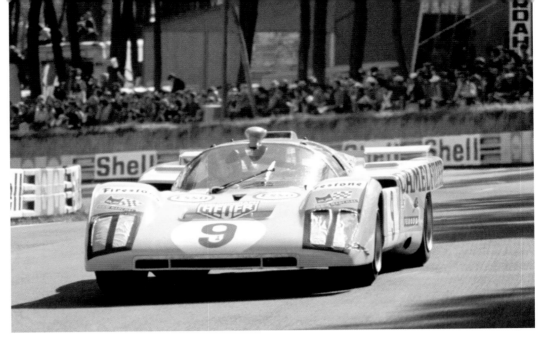

RIGHT Hughes de Fierlant/Alain de Cadenet, driving the #9 Jacques Swaters-entered 512 M (chassis 1030), were forced to retire from the 1971 Le Mans race at around half-distance with gearbox problems. *(LAT)*

the end of the race a rear shock absorber top had broken off, and the shock absorber had gone up into the shift rod and tried to shift the car into another gear while it was already in gear. As a result one of the gears wasn't working correctly, and I don't know if it can be attributed to that or not, but the ring and pinion gear broke in the gearbox. With about 15 minutes to go the car came in, and I can remember when it came into the pits you could hear it go …mmmm clunk…mmmm clunk as it grabbed the ring and pinion, and the car would move forward a bit each time. But you have to still be running at the end at Le Mans to qualify, so I kept the car in the pits for about 12 minutes or so, and then I sent it out for the last

lap, and we finished third behind two Porsche 917s. When we got it back to Connecticut and opened it up, there were just three teeth left on the ring gear and one on the pinion. It probably wouldn't have made another lap!'

The result must have been one of the most enjoyable and memorable times of his racing life. 'It was everything! Tony was a wonderful co-driver. I could count on him, because when I got out of the car I didn't feel as though I was handing over to somebody who was going to damage it in any way. In those days, of course, we only had two drivers per car. It was really wonderful. The race went incredibly well for us, and we were once again the first Ferrari home, which was a source of great pride to me.'

BELOW Finishing on the podium in the 1971 Le Mans 24-Hour race was a dream for Sam Posey/Tony Adamowicz in the #12 NART/Chinetti Ferrari 512 M (chassis 1020). *(LAT)*

Finishing on the podium at Le Mans would normally be the crowning glory for most drivers, but Sam Posey was anxious. 'Actually I didn't enjoy it very much because I was afraid we were going to be disqualified,' he explained. 'There was a rule that you had to do your last lap within a certain percentage of your fastest lap, and the rear end of our car was shot to pieces – Tony had to coax it around, and it wasn't fast enough to satisfy that rule. So I thought they were going to take our trophy away, so I didn't enjoy that moment very much. But they didn't impose that disqualification rule and our third-place finish stood.'

Österreichring 1,000km
27 June 1971

Despite the fact that Porsche had already clinched the World Championship, the John Wyer team wanted to assert its position in the racing world, and there was still the small matter of beating those pesky Alfa Romeos. Consequently Porsche cars, both prototype and GT, accounted for 14 of the 23 starters in a much reduced field. If truth be told, the top drivers would probably rather have had their teeth pulled than miss an opportunity to prove their superiority over their rivals.

On the grid were three Ferrari 512s, two of them well-known competitors comprising the José Juncadella car (chassis 1002) and that campaigned by Herbert Müller (chassis 1044). The third car, entered by Brescia Corse (chassis 1024) and driven by Marsilio Pasotti/Mario Casoni, was the ex-Chinetti 512 S that had been converted to M-spec. The three Ferraris occupied positions five, nine and twelve on the starting grid.

In the early stages the Herbert Müller/René Herzog Ferrari rose as high as third place but succumbed to the pressures of Helmut Marko's Porsche 917. Unfortunately, the Müller and Juncadella 512s were involved in separate accidents, but when the chequered flag came down it was the Brescia Corse Ferrari that was classified in fourth place.

200 Miles of Nürnberg, Norisring
11 July 1971

Pedro Rodríguez was scheduled to drive a BRM-Chevrolet P167 in this event, but just before the race the car's engine blew while

testing. Targa Florio teammate and friend Herbert Müller offered Rodríguez his Ferrari 512 M (chassis 1008) for the race, which he duly accepted. Rodríguez was placed second on the grid, but after just 11 laps he was forced into the wall by a slower car, and the #26 Ferrari crashed and burst into flames, killing him. This tragic incident was just two weeks after the Austrian race and a week before the British GP.

Watkins Glen 6-Hours
24/25 July 1971

The Watkins Glen 6-Hours would be the final time that the Group 5 race cars would be seen in anger in the World Championships. In a race that see-sawed between Ferrari, Porsche and Alfa Romeo it was perhaps inevitable that Porsche would come out on top, as the 917s had been dominant all year.

Lined up at the start were four Ferrari 512s, three Porsche 917s of which two were the John Wyer works cars, a pair of Alfa Romeo 33/3s and a single works Ferrari 312 PB. The Ferrari 512 M of Gregg Young/Jim Adams didn't make the start due to a fuel leak. It was no doubt a surprise to many – with the possible exception of the driver himself – when Mark Donohue placed the #6 Penske/Sunoco Ferrari on pole with a time of 1:07.74, almost a full second ahead of the works Porsche 917 driven by Jo Siffert/Gijs van Lennep.

Woody Woodard recalled, 'There were two races at Watkins Glen – first the six-hour enduro and then the Can-Am. In the first race we sat on pole. At the start Mark pulled away from

ABOVE Back at base, the #14 Chinetti car (chassis 1006) driven by Masten Gregory and George Eaton in the 1971 Le Mans 24-Hours is stripped down and overhauled. The car retired early in the race due to fuel problems. *(François Sicard Collection)*

ABOVE Mark Donohue
speeds away from pole
position in the Watkins
Glen 6-Hours on 24
July 1971. However,
his race in the #6
Penske Sunoco Ferrari
512 M would last only
53 laps. (LAT)

the others, but after about 50 laps the steering knuckle on the left upright separated. Mark just pulled off to the side with only one-wheel steer, and he sat there and watched the end of the race. We repaired it for the Can-Am race.'

The #48 Herbert Müller/George Eaton Ferrari (chassis 1044) was out after 17 laps because of an accident, and the #14 Sam Posey/Ronnie Bucknum Chinetti Ferrari (chassis 1020) retired on lap 126 with electrical problems. Together with the Donohue car, this meant that three of the four Ferrari 512s were out of the running before the halfway mark. This left just the #63 Jacques Swaters-entered car of Alain de Cadenet/Lothar Motschenbacher (chassis 1030) still in the race. Having started from tenth place on the grid, the Belgian Ferrari finished in a credible fourth place overall.

'That was probably another weak link in the 512, by the way,' said Woodard. 'Mark and I were talking about it when we first got the car, that it didn't quite look strong enough, because it was just a tapered-down steel fixture that screwed into the aluminium upright. It *looked* like it might have been a weak link, and anyway it did fail. In the Can-Am race Mark qualified fifth, substantially ahead of a number of big-block Chevrolet Can-Am cars, but the engine failed at about the halfway point. The Ferrari was sold right afterwards because we were taking delivery of the Siffert Porsche 917 Can-Am Spider.'

Starting from tenth on the Can-Am grid, the Sam Posey Chinetti-entered Ferrari gave a good account of itself, finishing in sixth place overall against some much bigger-engined cars. Sam Posey recalled, 'What happened there was we dropped out of the six-hour with an electrical problem at about half-distance while running second. So I went to Mr Chinetti and I said we should enter the Can-Am, because the car was running great. We'd only put three hours on it, and I said the Can-Am only takes two hours, so we should be fine. He agreed, and so I said, "Now, as for the prize money we'll split it," and he said that was fine too. So I really got into the race and I did well. Donohue beat me in the class, but only by a small margin.

'And so I went to Mr Chinetti after the race and I said to him, "Here's the prize money. We've just won $20,000. Will you give me a cheque?" He said, "I've never paid a driver that much, and I'm not going to pay you that much now." He was really steamed. So I said, "But we had a deal." So he said, "I'm sorry, I'm not going to pay you," but he paid me about $8,000 or something. But that was a wonderful race for me.'

Motor racing summary

There is no doubt in the minds of those interviewed who were involved one way or another with the Ferrari 512 at the time, that,

despite enormous promise, it just didn't achieve its full potential. Most cite as the cause the fact that Ferrari just dropped all further development and support for the car, which was a great pity on several levels. Firstly, the factory had obviously invested no small amount of financial resources and manpower into creating the race car in the first place. To then just drop it after a year, in a manner that suggested the company wasn't even interested, is somewhat beyond comprehension. Secondly, the damage to a company's reputation that an ill-performing race car can cause is something that a name like Ferrari would surely have wanted to avoid. Thirdly, the financial and marketing mileage that can be gained through even limited development can be fairly substantial, as witnessed by what Porsche did with the 917 in the Interserie and Can-Am series.

Woody Woodard said that chassis 1040 only raced five times in 1971 – at the Daytona 24-Hours, Sebring 12-Hours, Le Mans 24-Hours, Watkins Glen 6-Hours and Watkins Glen Can-Am (the last two races on the same weekend). He summarised his experience with it thus: 'In those five races chassis 1040 never won a thing. It was always fast and it was always the best-looking car at the racetrack, and I believe that, as a result of our meticulous preparation, it's what brought us to the attention of Porsche, which resulted in us getting the

Can-Am 917 for the next two years.' Certainly in a world where almost all Ferraris were red, the Penske Ferrari was conspicuous because of its distinctive Sunoco blue/yellow branding, and it's probably the best-known Ferrari sports racer of all time never to have won anything.

In general the 512 was a car that was full of promise, and as such probably the company's biggest disappointment. When asked how he felt about Ferrari withdrawing support from the 512 programme, Mauro Forghieri answered, 'I was very upset, but it was necessary to move to a new, smaller sports car. Of course, the decision by Ferrari was due to economical reasons as well.'

The 512 project had been rushed from drawing board to final product in just a few months. One could not say after two seasons of disappointing results that the 512 rewrote the record books, so how did the factory view its achievements? Forghieri was upbeat in his response: 'We saw it as totally positive because we were able to beat the 917 in Zeltweg, Austria, [before electrical problems sidelined the Ickx car] and at the end of the season in South Africa.'

So, with the benefit of hindsight, in what way could the 512 have been improved to achieve better results? Forghieri again: 'More torque, less weight, and an aerodynamic package with less drag.'

ABOVE The 512 M was generally outclassed in the Can-Am races. Here the #14 Ferrari (chassis 1020) driven by Sam Posey is overtaken at Watkins Glen by the winning #7 McLaren M8F of Peter Revson on 25 July 1971. The Ferrari finished a creditable sixth. *(LAT)*

'Due to the late decision to proceed with the 512 S, we were not able to put it through the usual wind tunnel test and road tests. Even in Sicily, where we did some testing, the winter that year was very bad.'

— Mauro Forghieri

Chapter Two

Anatomy of the Ferrari 512

Fortunately for Ferrari, they didn't need to reinvent the wheel when it came to developing the 512 S. With such vast racing experience and knowledge at their disposal, the 512 was always going to be a strong contender. The question was whether it could pack enough of a punch to match, and beat, the Porsche 917. Quite aside from the pressures of running their Formula 1 team, Ferrari didn't give sufficient time to the development of the 512.

OPPOSITE A close-up view of the Ferrari's large 5-litre V12 engine. *(Author)*

To say that the Ferrari 512 was a rushed job is to do the company and the engineers who worked on the project a grave disservice. It might be more accurate to say that the car was underdeveloped. As a company, Ferrari had enough experience on a wide range of fronts to draw from, so Mauro Forghieri had a good idea of what was needed.

There is no question that Enzo was put under pressure by Porsche in 1968, because motor racing meant everything to him. Being a small company, running a high-profile race team – or in his case teams – was an expensive business, and added to this was the problem of industrial unrest at the beginning of 1970. Developing new cars to satisfy the changing class requirements was crippling, and not only did he face the prospect of the new 3-litre class for 1972 but he was also wrong-footed by his adversary from Stuttgart, which didn't please him.

Mauro Forghieri recalled, 'The metal workers' strike really affected us, especially during the design phase of the 512, because the draughtsmen and the mechanics were forced to stay out of the factory.'

The 512 S was a Group 5 endurance racing car. Its one purpose in life was to beat the Porsche 917. The fact that it didn't was not due to any inherent weakness in the car's design or mechanical make-up. It is, however, true that the 512 didn't add many trophies to the Ferrari cabinet, but that was more a result of circumstance and racing incidents than defective design or engineering.

The 512 S arrived at the party a little late, and with insufficient test miles behind it, which is why the Porsche, with almost a full season of racing behind it, was superior. It was also during the 1969 season that the Porsche was turned from a widow-maker into the most fearsomely successful race car to date. Ferrari had undoubtedly been caught off-guard by Porsche's very quick reaction to the FIA's rule changes for the season. Despite the 917's early aerodynamic difficulties, Enzo Ferrari knew that his rivals would iron out their problems, and that before long they would have a winner on their hands, so he couldn't afford to sit idly by and watch as his main rival grabbed the limelight. Ferrari instead delivered a 512 S to the track full of promise, but rather short on development.

The origins of the 512's 60° V12 engine can be traced back as far as the 375 Plus from 1954, a 4.9-litre sports car whose engine was in turn derived from the 1950 4.5-litre Formula 1 Ferrari 375 racer. This magnificent engine was the work of the talented Ferrari engineer Aurelio Lampredi, and allowed progressive increases in

capacity while retaining solid reliability. Although the 512 had no immediate predecessor, Mauro Forghieri admitted that it 'was derived a little bit from the 612 Can-Am car', but endurance racing brought with it an altogether different set of survival criteria.

But why was the development on the 512 started so late in the day, and what prompted Ferrari to change his mind? Mauro Forghieri offered this explanation: 'It was partially because we were so involved in Formula 1, but discussions concerning the 512 started in 1969.' Such was the level of competition from the Porsches, that Ferrari probably learned more about their new 512 in that first race at Daytona than they'd done in the few months of hurried testing prior to the 1970 season.

Even though the 512 was more powerful

ABOVE **Leading the pack during a Group 5 demonstration run at the Goodwood 74th Members' Meeting in March 2016 is the #7 Ferrari of Nick Mason, followed by the green Lola of David Piper with the famous Le Mans-winning #23 Porsche 917. With a trio of similar cars in the background, this could have been a scene from 1971.** *(Simon Hildrew)*

LEFT **Set against the superb Gloucestershire countryside, the Nick Mason chassis 1026 512 S paints a handsome picture. The 512 S had twin driving-lights in the nose, the most obvious feature that differentiates it from the 512 M.** *(Author)*

than the Porsche 917, it lost out to the Porsche in most of the 1970 races, and also most of the 1971 races. With the benefit of hindsight, one might have expected the 512 to have been a better all-rounder than the Porsche, as Ferrari would have been able to learn from some of the mistakes made by their German rivals. But as Forghieri explained, 'Due to the late decision to proceed with the 512 S, we weren't able to put it through the usual wind tunnel test and road tests. Even in Sicily, where we did some testing, the winter that year was very bad.' It was therefore largely left up to the teams to do their own testing at the track, and in competition. If the 512 S had the luxury of limited testing, the 512 M had to undergo its testing entirely on the racetrack, at the Kyalami 9-Hours in November 1970 to be precise.

Body and design

Unlike so many of Ferrari's classic road and race car designs, Pininfarina had nothing to do with the 512 programme. 'Our internal motor sport design bureau was responsible for everything,' confirmed Forghieri. 'I was the project manager as usual, but I had very good draughtsmen and engineers. The drawings were based simply on personal experience and calculations arising from statistical data.'

The starting point for the design of the 512 S and 512 M was the windscreen, which in Group 5 was dictated by the regulations for that category. Casoli designed the body, and the Turinese boatbuilders Cigala & Bertinetti were contracted to fabricate these. For the first time in Ferrari's history body panels were made from fibreglass, the nose, tail section and doors all being finished in fibreglass and attached directly to the centre section. The formers for these were supplied by Ferrari to Cigala & Bertinetti in hand-beaten aluminium.

The minimum weight of the car was as specified on the Recognition Form, the official form used by the FIA for the initial approval of a race car and for homologation purposes. That weight measurement should include a spare wheel equal to the size of at least two of the four wheels fitted to the car. The weight specified on the form was measured with most liquid tanks full, including the oil tank, cooling,

BELOW The 512 S had a similar-looking tail end to that of the 917 K, with short stubby bodywork and two distinct wing sections, one either side of the central valley. *(Author)*

braking and heating (if fitted) but excluding the fuel tank.

'Mr Taddei, head of the internal construction department, was responsible for the assembly of the 512,' said Forghieri, 'and the component parts were fabricated by our machine tool department, of which I was the head on a project like this.' Gherardo Fantuzzi, one of Ferrari's favoured body constructors, was contracted to build certain body panels.

Drawing some inspiration from and influenced by stable contemporaries such as the Ferrari 330 P4, 612 Can-Am and the 312 P, the 512 was always going to be a quality act. However, the regulations covering the Group 4 (later Group 5) racer were quite different. Article 289 (c) of the 1968 FIA Code specified that a Group 4 race car with a closed body must have two rigid doors, giving direct access to each seat, a regulation that was transferred to Group 5 in 1971. The door-locking mechanism had to be capable of operation from both inside and outside the vehicle.

Regarding the car's aerodynamics, Article 252 (m) stipulated that any specific part of the car that had an aerodynamic influence on its stability must be entirely and only mounted on the sprung part of the car, referring basically to the bodywork. The regulation required that any such aerodynamic device(s) should be firmly fixed whilst the car is in motion, which ruled out any such movable devices as were fitted to the Porsche 908 LH and the early 917 LH. On the Porsches, the rear horizontal winglets could be raised or lowered depending on the car's speed or while cornering, and although these were homologated by the FIA they were outlawed at Le Mans. Neither the safety roll bar nor any of the units associated with the functioning of the engine or transmission were allowed to have any aerodynamic effect, possibly by creating a vertical thrust. The leading edge of any aerofoil fixed to the front of the car could not be sharp.

Even Forghieri admitted that the 917 initially had better aerodynamics than the 512. 'We had no wind tunnel test model for the 512 S. We had to use a real car for the Pininfarina wind tunnel test. Track testing was done in the beginning using chassis 1010.'

Chinetti/NART driver Sam Posey said that the M was a much better car than the S in all areas, confirming that the development on the M

BELOW The 512 S was a handsome prototype sports racer, with an aggressive stance and a more modern profile than the 330 P4. *(Author)*

ABOVE As can be seen on the raised engine cover on this 512 S, the hot air exiting from the radiators would simply flow over the rear bodywork. (Author)

RIGHT The hot air exiting the radiators on the 512 M is channelled more purposefully towards the rear as it passes over the engine cover, adding to the rear downforce and improving the car's aerodynamics. (Author)

done at the factory over the winter of 1970 had really paid dividends. Forghieri smiled at this. 'Sam is very kind! The changes to the 512 M were mainly aerodynamic improvements, with a different weight ratio that resulted in less front-to-rear change, for improved stability. There was a noticeable reduction in interactive airflow, better radiator positioning and more downforce on the back. A reduction in the ground clearance helped create a more stable roll centre.'

The different weight ratio that resulted in less front-to-rear change refers to a reduced transfer of weight under braking and acceleration, which in turn resulted in improved stability. The noticeable reduction in interactive airflow is best explained by Emanuele Nicosia, designer in the Pininfarina advanced design studio between 1976 and 1985: 'This refers to the interaction of two different airflows, which, when they meet, create a field of messy air that is very difficult to manage. These two flows are the under panel

flow (water/oil radiators, engine and brakes) and the aerodynamic flow around the body. The improvements reduced the flow length in which these two flows met and created messy air.'

The nose radius of the 512 S is more rounded and has a pair of low-level driving lights mounted together in the centre. Either side of these lights is an air intake that collects cool air and feeds this to the front brakes. Each fender carries a large headlamp and the front section between the fenders and ahead of the windscreen is fairly flat and low, giving the driver an excellent forward field of vision.

The nose of the 512 M is more steeply inclined than on the S, and has also lost the centre lamps, having instead a lower, sharper edge. This restyling gave the 512 M a much cleaner-looking front end. The lower section is dominated by a full-width air intake divided into three scoops internally; the two outer air scoops still feed air to the brakes, while the centre section feeds air to a radiator that has its vent on the top side of the front bodywork, ahead of the windscreen. Some 512 Ss have small vertical fins that run over the top of fenders that help direct the airflow over the wheel arches towards the two large air intakes for the radiators, mounted behind the doors and just ahead of the rear wheels.

François Sicard, mechanic on the 512 S for Chinetti/NART, considered that the S 'looked like a frog, and it had big ears on the side for the air intakes. It was just ugly. The M, though, was much prettier, and much lighter than the S.' But those 'big ears' scoop ample quantities of air for the radiators mounted ahead of the rear wheels, and are certainly a prominent feature. Their presence is perhaps accentuated by the fact that the rear deck, or engine cover and associated bodywork, is raised all the way to

RIGHT This shows the NART Ferrari 512 M (chassis 1020) during a rebuild outside the Chinetti workshops in Greenwich, Connecticut. *(François Sicard Collection)*

BELOW Two vents located just in front of the windscreen fed cool air into the cockpit. The vent on the left fed fresh air to the driver while that on the right directed cool air up the inside of the windscreen. *(Author)*

the tail. The doors open forward on both the S and the M models, thereby creating easy access to the cabin for driver changes.

The 512 S was available in both Coupé and Spider form, but the 512 M came only in closed Coupé form. That said, several taller 512 M drivers had to have a bubble built into the roof to accommodate their helmet. Penske driver David Hobbs had this to say about the Sunoco 512 M: 'The worst thing was the seating. Mark Donohue was a bit shorter than me, so my legs were always jammed underneath the steering wheel and my head hit the roof a lot, especially at places like Sebring, which is very bumpy. My head would be just chattering against the roof, which is a little bit off-putting.' The doors on the Spider version simply ended at the top of the Perspex windows, as there was no frame to the top of the door.

Some 512 Ss use small exterior rear-view mirrors perched on top of thin stalks, while others have more chunky stalks, but there seems to be little commonality in this respect. The 512 M has larger, more aerodynamically shaped mirrors, almost flush-mounted on top of the fenders, although some teams and drivers preferred

LEFT With the bodywork removed, the two vents can be clearly seen. *(Author)*

FAR LEFT Some taller drivers insisted that the roof be modified to accommodate their helmet. A roof bulge can be seen on this 512 M, chassis 1002, just to the left of the roof mirror. *(Author)*

LEFT The 512 S featured sturdy mirror stalks. *(Author)*

BELOW The 512 M featured revised, shorter mirror stalks, as the rear bodywork was lower than on the 512 S. *(Author)*

to attach taller stalks on to which the mirror housings were then mounted. This did, though, depend on the driver's seating position, and on what rear-wing arrangement had been fitted. Because rearward vision is difficult anyway, most 512s had a roof-mounted mirror that the driver would look up into, giving a view back over the centre of the car. On the 512 M the mirror had to be offset to the left of the car, in order to see past the airbox that sat directly behind the driver.

A large engine cover, hinged just behind the cockpit, lifts as a big single unit, allowing

BELOW When fitted, the roof mirror on the 512 was extremely useful. *(Author)*

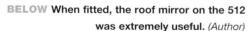

excellent access to the engine, gearbox and just about all the mechanicals. On the 512 S the engine cover separates along a line that runs horizontally more or less level with the tops of the rear tyres. Cars differed, but some S models feature a central transparent panel over the engine; others have a slatted section to aid hot air exiting from the engine bay. Other cars have slatted vents above and just behind the water radiators. On the 512 M, quite literally the whole back of the car lifts up as a single unit, which gives unrestricted access to everything mechanical, including the radiators.

On the 512 M a rather unsightly airbox was mounted above the 12 intake trumpets, which feeds air down into the inlet manifold. Some Ferrari commentators point out that the 512 S presents a better-looking silhouette as it doesn't have this rather awkward-looking airbox, the air being instead drawn down by way of a vortex created by the airflow over the top of the roof. The 512 M, on the other hand, produces more power as a result of more air being force-fed down in the inlet manifold, and as racing cars are meant to do just that, function had to take precedence over form.

At the bottom of the rear bodywork on the 512 S, a neat air scoop projects out just ahead of the rear wheels to collect and direct cool air to the brakes. On the 512 M this is slightly larger, and faired into the bodywork, and consequently looks much neater.

The tail ends of the two versions are quite different from each other. The engine cover of the 512 S is characterised by a central valley that's framed on either side by a pair of low vertical fins that extend rearwards. To the left and the right are short fixed-wing arrangements that serve as the rear aerofoil. The 512 M, on the other hand, has lower rear fenders that extend rearwards from the radiator intakes on either side of the car, at the tail end of which are

ABOVE Sitting on top of the trumpet stack of the 512 M was a prominent fibreglass air scoop, effective but not universally loved. *(Author)*

LEFT The airbox on the 512 S Spider sat below the roof line, and with the roof panel removed the air passed over the windscreen, through the cockpit and into the airbox. *(Don Heiny, courtesy of RM Sotheby's)*

BELOW On the 512 S, a discreet scoop located just ahead of the rear wheel fed cool air to the brakes. *(Don Heiny, courtesy of RM Sotheby's)*

ABOVE The rearward-sloping surface of the front fender was slatted to allow additional hot air to escape from the inner wheel arch area. *(Author)*

ABOVE RIGHT The air intake that fed cool air to the brakes on the 512 M sat flush with the bodywork and was therefore more streamlined. While it was just as effective, it didn't offer any wind resistance like the scoop on the 512 S did. *(Author)*

BELOW The Herbert Müller/Mike Parkes Ferrari 512 S (chassis 1016) featured a *Coda Lunga*, or long-tail body. *(LAT)*

small adjustable winglets. The central bodywork over the engine appears raised due to the lower fenders, and is a well fashioned and integrated extension of the cockpit, creating a more pleasing and aerodynamic shape. In some ways the final iteration of the 512 M more closely resembled the rear of the Porsche 917 K.

There is always an exception to the norm, and the Penske Sunoco 512 M was fitted with a full-width rear wing. Don Cox, Penske's chief engineer, explained why: 'I had been working on Chaparrals for three years at the point when I left

Chevrolet in the fall of 1969, so I was keen on putting a wing on everything because we knew what the advantages would be. But a lot of people hadn't figured that out yet, even though the Chaparrals started running wings in 1967.'

For the 1970 Le Mans, the 512 S could be fitted with a longer tail section, similar to that seen on the Porsche 908 LH and 917 LH. It basically consisted of an extended section of bodywork that was gradually tapered towards the tail, and featured a pair of stubby vertical fins mounted right at the back end. A shallow full-width, wrap-around aerofoil or wing finished off the tail, its ends angled downwards on the flanks of the rear fender. The name *Coda Lunga* was given to the long tail modification.

When asked in what way he thought the 512 could have been improved, apart from wanting more power, Forghieri answered, 'Better weight distribution, and better aerodynamics with lower drag.'

ABOVE The rear bodywork of the Ferrari 512 S (in this instance chassis 1006) was higher that the M-spec version. *(Don Heiny, courtesy of RM Sotheby's)*

LEFT By installing new, revised radiators, the rear bodywork of the 512 M (chassis 1024 is shown) was somewhat lower than on the S. *(Don Heiny, courtesy of RM Sotheby's)*

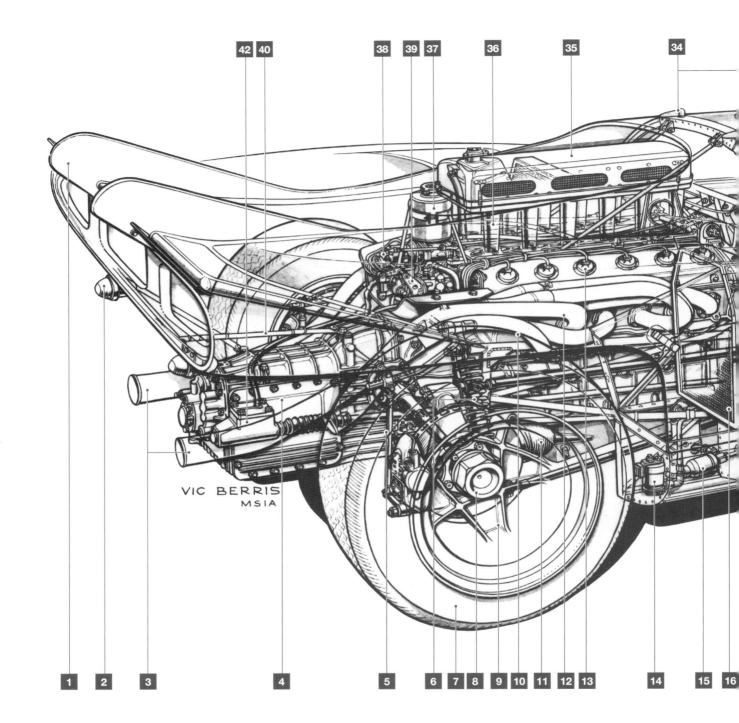

Cutaway of Ferrari 512 S. *(LAT)*

1 Rear wing structure
2 Rear light (Carello)
3 Exhaust pipes
4 Five-speed gearbox
5 Rear suspension drop-link
6 Rear spring and shock-absorber
7 Rear tyre – 6.00/14.50 x 15

8 80mm wheel nut
9 Campagnolo wheel rim
10 5-litre V12 engine
11 Cooling duct for rear brakes
12 Exhaust branch
13 Spark plug rain cap
14 Fuel lift pump

15 Fuel filter
16 Radiator for engine cooling
17 Fuel collector tank
18 Aluminium sill covering fuel bladder
19 Gear shift lever
20 Gear shift lever housing
21 Clutch and brake master cylinder

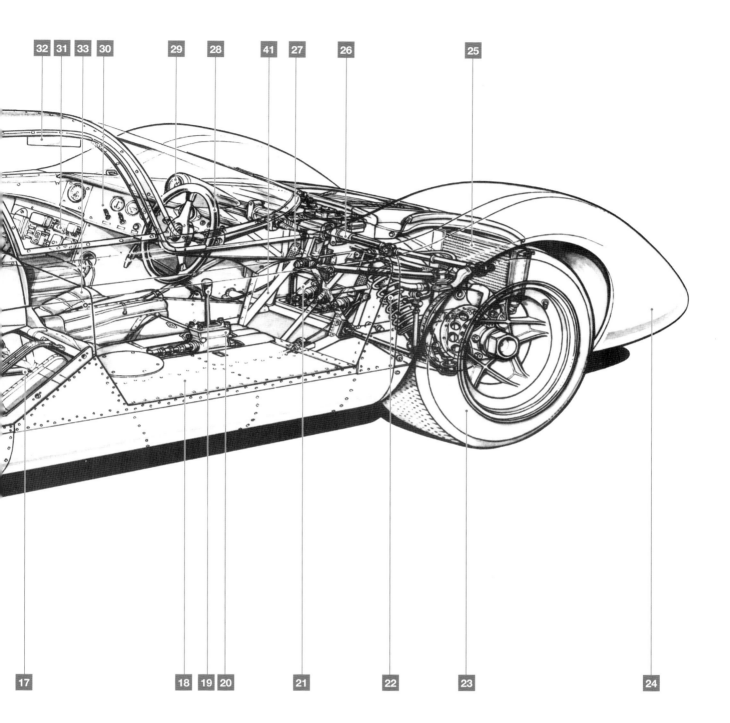

22 Front spring and shock-absorber

23 Front tyre – 4.75/11.50 x 15

24 Front bodywork

25 Oil cooler radiator

26 Steering rack

27 Clutch pedal

28 Momo steering wheel

29 Cool air outlet for driver

30 Dashboard

31 Interior rear view mirror

32 Fuses and electrics board

33 Driver's seat

34 Engine cover hinges

35 Air collector box

36 One of twelve trumpets

37 Engine coolant header tank

38 Distributor

39 Fuel metering unit

40 Rear bodywork support

41 Spaceframe support

42 Gear selector housing

RIGHT On either side of the car, beneath the broad aluminium panel covering the sill and protected by the car's tubular frame, were two 60-litre fuel bladders. *(Author)*

Chassis

Ferrari commenced its chassis numbering sequence from number 1002 and ran up to number 1050. Chassis number 1000 was omitted, and only even numbers were used – for example 1002, 1004, 1006, 1008 etc, up to 1050, thereby totalling 25 cars.

The 512's chassis, developed originally from the Ferrari 330 P4, was standard Ferrari construction of the day. It has even been suggested that the 512 had the same chassis as the 612 P Can-Am car, but with a different body. Whatever origins the 512 had, it wasn't a new chassis, as the factory would not have had the time to create an altogether new spaceframe.

With this in mind, the spaceframe consisted of tubular steel tubing reinforced with aluminium sheet riveted to the centre section. This forms a semi-monocoque structure and spaceframe, with stressed-alloy panelling around the cockpit area. The front and rear suspensions are mounted on a subframe while the engine is used as a stressed component of the structure. While this may be a heavy construction, the assembly method was well known to Ferrari personnel and therefore fairly easy for the workers to fabricate. It is estimated that the 512's steel chassis weighed about 100kg more than the aluminium multi-tubular framework of the Porsche 917, which is said to have weighed just 46kg, although it did suffer with rigidity issues.

CENTRE This shows the bulkhead, air vent intake, holes for the left and right fuel fillers and the general monocoque structure forming the cockpit of NART 512 M chassis 1020. *(François Sicard Collection)*

According to Forghieri, Maioli and Farina designed the chassis, and once the design was complete the job of building the required quota of chassis was given to the Vaccari workshop in Modena. William Vaccari had been working for Maserati since 1940, but he was enticed away by none other than Enzo Ferrari, and persuaded to open his own workshop. Naturally Vaccari was to supply only Ferrari with chassis, but such was his standard of workmanship that Enzo was prepared to appoint him as his preferred supplier. 'Sometimes, though,' Forghieri added, 'we got them from Giancarlo Guerra.' It should be mentioned that Guerra, an associate of Sergio Scaglietti, is credited with fashioning some of Ferrari's most celebrated creations, such as the Ferrari 250 Testarossa,

BELOW This photograph shows the basic spaceframe structure of the rear of NART 512 M chassis 1020. On the left and right are the aluminium 'pods' in which the engine cooling radiators were located. *(François Sicard Collection)*

250GT Spider California, 250 GTO, 275 GTB and 365 GTB/4 Daytona.

Forghieri confirmed that chassis building only commenced around the end of September 1969, the 25 units taking around three months to complete. The homologation inspection took place in January 1970, when Ferrari presented 17 complete cars plus full sets of component parts to build the remaining eight cars. Although, as we have seen, Porsche's presentation of just three completed 917s with the remainder in various stages of completion didn't receive the inspectors' approval, Enzo Ferrari was clearly more persuasive. Following homologation the first batch of 512s was hastily air-freighted to the USA for the Daytona 24-Hour race.

Reports as to how many 512s were eventually completed vary, some saying 17 and

ABOVE The rear bodywork was supported by a light frame that was mounted on the rear of the gearbox. (Author)

BELOW This photograph showing the rear of a 512 M reveals the mounting points for the bodywork support frame, and also the rear towing loop, which is attached to the rear end of the gearbox. (Don Heiny, courtesy of RM Sotheby's)

some saying 19. The remaining spare parts were used in the rebuilding of crashed cars. One chassis was given to Pininfarina, where designer Paolo Martin created the striking 512 S Modulo concept car that was unveiled at the 1970 Geneva Motor Show.

Engine

The FIA Sporting Code divided engine capacities across all Groups into 13 different class groupings in which various cars would compete on the international stage. With reference to this list, the Ferrari 512 fell into Class 12, which covered the cylinder capacity class for cars between 3,000cc and 5,000cc.

The naturally aspirated 5-litre Ferrari 512 engine came from the same castings as the 6.9-litre Can-Am engine, and being reduced to just 4,994cc it would have been almost bulletproof. As such, it replicated its bigger brother in its classic 60° V12 layout, with four camshafts operating 48 valves. In fact, the origins of the engine architecture can be traced back even further, to the 1950 4.5-litre Formula 1 375 race car, which was upgraded in 1954 to 4,954cc for the 375 Plus sports car. 'The new engine was based on an existing, modified unit which was first used in an early F1 car that featured screwed-in liners,' explained Forghieri.

BELOW Access to the engine, gearbox and most mechanicals was relatively easy. *(Author)*

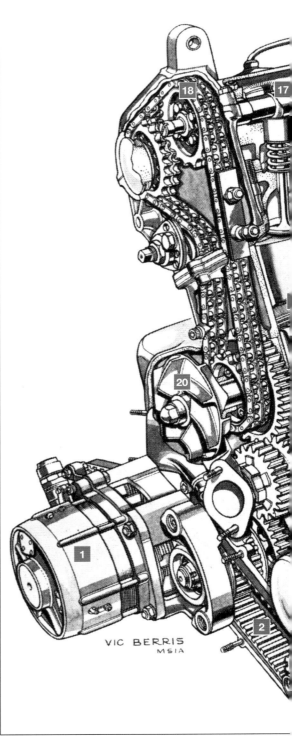

VIC BERRIS
MSIA

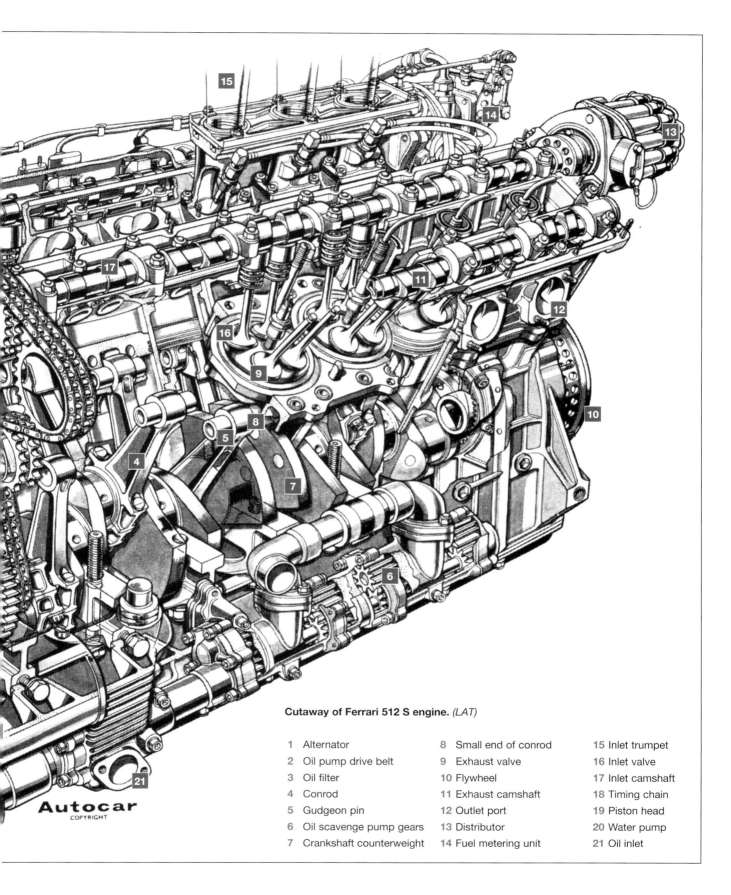

Cutaway of Ferrari 512 S engine. *(LAT)*

1	Alternator	8	Small end of conrod	15	Inlet trumpet
2	Oil pump drive belt	9	Exhaust valve	16	Inlet valve
3	Oil filter	10	Flywheel	17	Inlet camshaft
4	Conrod	11	Exhaust camshaft	18	Timing chain
5	Gudgeon pin	12	Outlet port	19	Piston head
6	Oil scavenge pump gears	13	Distributor	20	Water pump
7	Crankshaft counterweight	14	Fuel metering unit	21	Oil inlet

Autocar
COPYRIGHT

ABOVE Protecting the distributor and other sensitive components from the high heat generated by the exhaust pipes was a heat shield with protective heat-resistant cloth. *(Author)*

BELOW The 12 trumpets stand proudly atop the engine. It may appear that the trumpets vary in length between the front and the back of the engine, but it's actually the airbox being slightly raised at the rear that creates this impression, as the trumps are all the same length. *(Author)*

'The 60° V12 engine was then increased to 84 x 74.5mm. Franco Rocchi was responsible for drawing up the draught of the engine, with help from Giacomo Caliri. Giancarlo Bussi in the test department was responsible for the engine development.'

Power-wise, the Ferrari engine initially put out 560bhp at 8,500rpm, which was the same as the 917 Porsche, although the Ferrari unit could be revved to 9,600rpm. Dimensionally, the engine measured 31.5 x 21.0 x 21.0 inches without the fuel injection fittings, and weighed in at 584lb. Internally referenced as the Type 261, the new engine used a Lucas fuel injection system that fed fuel into light alloy heads. The 512's compression ratio runs at 11.5:1 and the light-alloy heads feature four valves per cylinder, being operated by way of twin overhead camshafts per bank of cylinders. The cylinder firing order of the 5-litre engine is 1-7-5-11-3-9-6-12-2-8-4-10.

The engine is mounted longitudinally behind the cockpit in a mid-ship position, and forms a stressed member of the chassis. This was more or less the same as the Porsche unit, although the German engine, being air-cooled, featured an integral cooling system that in the Ferrari's

case still needed plumbing and radiators for cooling. The extra weight of the additional radiators and associated plumbing made the Ferrari heavier, which in turn negatively affected the car's power-to-weight ratio when compared with the Porsche 917.

When cold starting the 512 S, the cam on the fuel distributor should be rotated fully clockwise so as to enrich the mixture by the maximum amount possible. As the car was only fitted with a lightweight battery, it was recommended that an external heavy-duty battery be connected in parallel to assist with start-up. Should this still not be sufficient to get the engine started, a small amount of fuel can be sprayed into each intake trumpet. In really cold conditions it is even permissible to preheat the fuel distributor prior to the commencement of the starting procedure, in order to prevent the unit from seizing. In this event, hot water can be poured over the unit, or a hair dryer can be used to warm the distributor.

Once the engine has been successfully started and is running, it is important to run it at the lowest possible revs until the oil pressure has registered on the gauge. Intermittent blipping of the throttle is encouraged to avoid

fouling the plugs, but care should be taken not to exceed an oil pressure of $14kg/m^2$, or until the oil temperature has reached 60°C, as this could result in the failure of the oil cartridge. Once the engine has reached normal operating temperature, the fuel distributor cam can be dialled back to its normal running position. Ferrari recommended 10mm Champion GR 196 or Marchal 810 spark plugs.

The procedure for setting the timing on the

FERRARI 512 S TECHNICAL SPEC

Engine	Rear-mounted 60° V12, light alloy cylinder block and heads.
Timing gear	Four valves per cylinder, twin overhead camshafts per cylinder bank.
Bore and stroke	87 x 70mm.
Total displacement	4,993.53cc.
Compression ratio	11.5:1.
Firing order	1-7-5-11-3-9-6-12-2-8-4-10.
Ignition advance	34° BTDC.
Maximum power	550bhp at 8,500rpm.
Specific power	110.1bhp/litre.
Power/weight ratio	1.5kg/bhp.
Maximum torque	371.5029ft/lb at 5,500rpm.
Fuel	Lucas fuel injection.
Ignition	Single with one distributor.
Transmission	Multi-plate clutch, five-speed gearbox + reverse, ZF limited-slip differential.
Chassis	Semi-monocoque.
Front suspension	Independent, double wishbones, coil springs, dampers.
Rear suspension	Independent, double wishbones, coil springs, dampers.
Steering	Rack.
Wheelbase	2,400mm.
Overall length	4,060mm.
Overall width	2,000mm.
Height	972mm.
Front/rear track	1,518/1,511mm.
Kerb weight	840kg.
Front tyres	4.75 x 11.50/15.
Rear tyres	6.00 x 14.50/15.
Fuel tank	120 litres (2 x 60 litres).
Top speed	340kph (211.2mph).

ENGINE AND HEAD TORQUE SETTINGS

Cylinder head studs	11.06kg or 80ft/lb.
Main bearing caps – vertical	11.75kg or 85ft/lb.
Main bearing caps – horizontal	4.84kg or 35ft/lb.
Big ends and bolts	6.91kg or 50ft/lb.
Inlet valve clearance (cold)	0.15–0.20mm or 0.006–0.008in.
Exhaust valve clearance (cold)	0.45–0.50mm or 0.018–0.020in.

FERRARI 512 M TECHNICAL SPEC

Engine	Mid-rear-mounted 60° V12, light alloy cylinder block and heads.
Timing gear	Four valves per cylinder, twin overhead camshafts per cylinder bank.
Bore and stroke	87 x 70mm.
Total displacement	4,993.53cc.
Compression ratio	11.5:1.
Maximum power	610bhp at 9,000rpm.
Specific power	122.1bhp/litre.
Power/weight ratio	1.3kg/bhp.
Fuel	Lucas fuel injection.
Ignition	Single with one distributor.
Transmission	Multi-plate clutch, five-speed gearbox + reverse, ZF limited-slip differential.
Chassis	Semi-monocoque.
Front suspension	Independent, double wishbones, coil springs, dampers.
Rear suspension	Independent, double wishbones, coil springs, dampers.
Steering	Rack.
Wheelbase	2,400mm.
Front/rear track	1,518/1,511mm.
Kerb weight	815kg.
Front tyres	4.25 x 11.50/15.
Rear tyres	6.00 x 14.50/15.
Fuel tank	120 litres (2 x 60 litres).
Top speed	340kph (211.2mph).

ABOVE Oil could be replenished without lifting the large rear engine cover, as the oil filler cap was easily accessible through the bodywork. (*Author*)

ABOVE RIGHT The oil tank for the dry sump lubrication system was located behind the left-hand side radiator, just ahead of the rear wheel. (*Author*)

RIGHT Oil was piped to the oil coolers at the front of the vehicle and returned to the dry sump tank via the pipe seen here at the bottom of the radiator. (*Author*)

fuel distributor is somewhat more involved, as with the engine mounted in the car it's difficult to locate the TDC firing stroke of the number 1 cylinder. According to Ferrari the timing of the point of fuel injection isn't critical, and also isn't adjustable. The fuel distributor is fitted with a rotatable cam that has five pre-set positions, and turning the cam clockwise will enrich the mixture, while turning it anticlockwise will weaken the mixture across the whole operating range.

The engine lubrication system consists of a dry sump tank, located behind the cockpit on the left-hand side, and two scavenge pumps that return the oil to the tank. Oil is drawn from the dry sump tank and fed to the engine

RIGHT The distributor was protected from the heat generated by the exhaust by an insulated heat shield. (*Author*)

through a Fram filter by means of a single high-pressure pump. Two oil-cooling radiators are located on each side at the front of the car and the oil is fed to them and returned to the tank through oil lines that run down the right-hand side when looking at the car from the front.

The minimum oil pressure of 6.5kg/cm^2 (93lbs/in^2) at maximum revs should be maintained, but if this should drop it can be increased by adjusting the pressure relief valve fitted to the body of the pressure pump. Adjusting the valve clockwise increases the pressure. The oil tank has a capacity of 12 to 18 litres (2.65 to 4.0 imperial gallons). The oil recommended by Ferrari was Shell SC3; they also advised that both oil and Fram filter should be changed periodically, which is a bit like telling the team to put fuel in the fuel tank before a race.

The exhaust pipes, which in the Ferrari 512 exit at the rear of the car, were also governed by regulation. Article 253 (l) stipulated that the exhaust orifices should not be above 45cm or below 10cm from the ground, and should not extend more than 15cm beyond the rear bodywork.

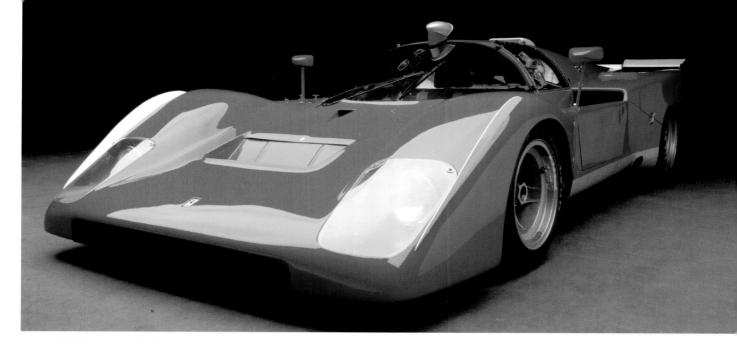

ABOVE On the 512 M the top of the radiator intake was level with the bottom of the driver's window. *(Don Heiny, courtesy of RM Sotheby's)*

Cooling system

On both the 512 S and the 512 M, the twin engine-cooling radiators are located on the sides of the car behind the large fuel tanks and ahead of the rear wheels. The cooling system consists of two separate circuits, one serving the left bank of cylinders and the other the right bank. It stands to reason, then, that each bank of cylinders and head has its own header tank, radiator and water pump.

The cooling system can be filled in one of two ways: either conventionally through one of the header tanks, which for this purpose were interconnected with each other; or under pressure via the pressure-feed valve located on the left-hand side of the car near the door. The cooling system is filled with a solution of water with 30% glycol added, thus increasing the operating range of the coolant and improving the cooling efficiency of the water. The radiator caps can withstand a pressure of 28.5–31.3lb/in^2.

RIGHT The 512 M had its dry sump oil tank located further inboard, which contributed to the car's improved handling over the S version, as more weight was concentrated in the centre of the vehicle. *(François Sicard Collection)*

LEFT The large air intakes on the 512 S were more prominent than on the 512 M. Here it can be seen that the top of the radiator intake was several inches above the level of the bottom of the driver's window. *(Author)*

LEFT On the 512 S the oil coolers were located on the left and the right of the car, as the S had a pair of driving lamps located in the centre front. *(Author)*

CENTRE The 512 M, on the other hand, had its twin oil coolers mounted in the middle of the car, and the air escaped up through a large single central vent. *(François Sicard Collection)*

Although the 512 S and 512 M both have their oil coolers located in the nose of the car, the S has them located on the left and right of the body whereas the 512 M has them located together in the centre, which brings the weight inboard of the wheels and therefore improves the car's roll centre of gravity. No doubt this relocation of the radiators played a key role in improving the handling of the 512 M.

Transmission

Forghieri says that Walter Salvarani was responsible for the draught design of the gearbox. The 512 S is fitted with a gearbox that was developed in-house and features five forward gears and a reverse gear. This is bolted to the rear of the engine and drives the rear wheels through a multi-plate clutch. The gearbox oil is pressure-fed from a pump driven by the input shaft and draws its oil (Shell 6909) from the gearbox sump.

Changing the gear ratios requires a change of the crown wheel and pinion. A change to the fifth gear only requires the removal of the rear cover, but care needs to be exercised here, as the rear cover also contains the outer race of the rear roller bearing for the input and output shafts. It's advisable to periodically overhaul the gearbox and to replace the ball and roller races, while at the same time crack-checking all the gears.

For satisfactory operation of the gearbox, it is important that the gear change linkage is accurately adjusted. With the gearbox at normal working temperature, and with the car in neutral, the gear lever should be exactly in the middle of the gate, in the fore and aft plane. The lever should also be checked for its lateral positioning by ensuring that the same clearance exists between the side of the lever and the side of the

RIGHT The gear lever sat in the sill area, above the fuel bladder, and fell comfortably to hand for the driver. *(Author)*

512 S SPEEDS USING DIFFERENT RING AND PINION SETS

(Data source: Ferrari 512 S workshop manual.)

	Speed in kph @ 8,000rpm	Speed in kph @ 8,500rpm
Ring and pinion gear set 8/34		
1st gear	90	97.5
2nd gear	132	140
3rd gear	175	181
4th gear	215	227.5
5th gear	250	265
Ring and pinion gear set 9/34		
1st gear	102.5	107.5
2nd gear	147.5	155
3rd gear	190	200
4th gear	237.5	250
5th gear	275	292.5
Ring and pinion gear set 10/34		
1st gear	112.5	120
2nd gear	162.5	172.5
3rd gear	212.5	222.5
4th gear	262.5	277.5
5th gear	310	325
Ring and pinion gear set 11/35		
1st gear	120	127.5
2nd gear	175	185
3rd gear	225	237.5
4th gear	285	300
5th gear	330	347.5

512 M SPEEDS USING DIFFERENT RING AND PINION SETS

Daytona and Le Mans preferred gear sets

(Data source: Ferrari 512 M workshop manual.)

Ring and pinion gear set 9/34		
1st gear	102.5	110
2nd gear	147.5	155
3rd gear	190	200
4th gear	237.5	250
5th gear	277.5	292.5
Ring and pinion gear set 10/34		
1st gear	112.5	120
2nd gear	162.5	172.5
3rd gear	210	222.5
4th gear	265	277.5
5th gear	310	325

turret in the plane of both fourth and fifth gears, and also in the plane of first and reverse.

In the ratios on the left ('8/34', '9/34' etc), the figure '8' refers to the number of teeth on the pinion and the number '34' is the number of teeth on the ring. François Sicard explained why you would use the different ring and pinion gear sets: '8/34 is a very low gear, that you would use for Sebring, Zolder or Spa. The long gears, the 10/34, you would use for Le Mans or

ABOVE Adjusting the gear linkage required skill and experience. This adjustment was located on the selector shaft immediately behind the gear lever. *(Author)*

LEFT This image shows the position of the gear lever in the general layout of the cockpit. *(Author)*

Daytona.' From this explanation, it can be seen that the higher ring and pinion gear sets, like the 10/34, provide a higher top speed, which is desirable at faster circuits, while the lower ratio of 8/34 would give quicker acceleration, which is better-suited to shorter circuits, where acceleration out of corners is more important than long, sustained top speeds. With the 512 M fitted with the longest gear ratio set, namely the 11/35, the theoretical top speed is just short of 350kph, but many factors play into these figures, such as wind, driver weight, circuit traffic and, of course, different circuits.

The engine revolutions and speeds in the tables have been calculated using a 26.2in diameter rear tyre, and this is important, because the tyres from different manufacturers have different dimensions. Sicard again: 'You make a mark on the ground and a mark on the tyre, then you roll the wheel forward until the mark is again in the same position. Then you measure that distance and from that you can calculate the speed of the car, because sometimes some people might use a Firestone while others use Goodyear tyres, and you could have a difference of maybe four or five inches in one revolution of the tyre, and that makes a difference too.'

Woody Woodard, Penske's chief mechanic,

outlined a weak link in the operation of the gearbox: 'The actual shift lever was typical Ferrari with the chrome fingered gate, but if there was a weak link on that car it was the shift linkage. At the back of the linkage there were multiple universal joints, but where it connected to the shaft that went into the transmission there was just a stud with two nuts, so it was very difficult to get a perfect alignment. A wide aluminium panel covered the top of the fuel bladder, and the shift lever was in the left front of that panel, down in a hole. That's why the right bladder was slightly smaller than the left, to make room for the shift linkage that was actually down inside the fuel bladder area. And typically I had to remind both drivers [Donohue and Hobbs] to be very careful with shifting.'

The 512 S is fitted with a three-plate multi-disc sintered clutch, the recommended brand being Borg & Beck CP 2014. At least 20mm or ¾in free travel should be maintained on the clutch pedal, since less could result in the clutch slipping. Drivers were advised not to slip the clutch on take-off as this would result in a high wear rate, creating unnecessary heating of the plates and deformation of the clutch. The differential is a ZF unit and incorporates a limited slip device.

BELOW The rear of the gearbox protruded beyond the rear tyres but was covered by the bodywork. This still left the gearbox vulnerable to damage as neither the body nor the flimsy frame holding it up offered any form of protection. *(RM Sotheby's)*

Steering and suspension

Steering was by rack and pinion. It was laid down in Article 253 (a) of the regulations that cars in Class A should have a maximum turning circle radius of 6.75m. Drivers were critical of the 512 S's ability to turn easily, saying that it was too heavy, but some repositioning of suspension points made the 512 M much easier in this respect.

Bob Houghton, well-known Ferrari restorer, explained why the steering was so heavy: 'Just the way they had the geometry and the wishbone and castor set up made the steering heavy, and if you ask any 512 driver, they'll tell you that the steering was *very* heavy. This was a result of the upright leaning forward from the vertical by about 4°, which was quite a lot.' Most modern cars have a positive castor, which means that the castor angle of the upright leans backward from the vertical, and as a self-centring mechanism the steering wheel will naturally return to the centre position. A negative castor will require greater input from the driver in turning the steering wheel into a corner, and more effort will again be required when exiting the corner as the wheels lack the tendency to return to the centre position. This,

ABOVE A Momo steering wheel is what one could expect to find in the typical 512 cockpit. *(Author)*

together with its very wide tyres, gave the 512 its heavy steering and ensured that the driver had a busy time in the cockpit.

After long-distance races, Ferrari teams

LEFT The outboard end of the steering rod is connected to the top of the hub by means of a rose joint. The inboard end of the steering rod is connected to the steering rack. *(Author)*

BELOW Visible just in front of the bulkhead is the steering rack. *(Author)*

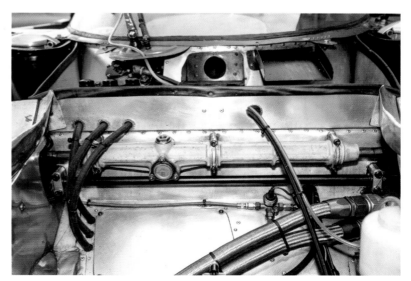

were advised to check that all pivot points and linkages were in good order, and that the front wheels were perfectly balanced. The steering system should also be devoid of play or stiffness and the steering box oil levels should be checked regularly and topped up with Shell Dentax 140.

The independent Ferrari 512 S suspension comprises upper and lower transverse wishbones and co-axial dampers and coil springs. It is fitted with double-acting adjustable Koni shock absorbers, on which both the compression and extension settings are adjustable with the shock absorbers still in place on the car. The recommended shock absorber settings should be: front 220kg extension, 70kg compression; rear 260kg extension, 90kg compression.

Adjusting the compression setting is achieved by rotating the adjustment knob on the lower part of the shock absorber clockwise to stiffen it, and anticlockwise to soften it. To adjust the extension setting, the perforated disc on the top of the shock absorber is rotated horizontally in a clockwise direction to soften the action, or anti-clockwise to stiffen it. The ride height of the vehicle can also be adjusted on the shock absorbers by slackening the two threaded ring nuts and then rotating these appropriately up or down, before tightening them again. The vehicle's height above the ground should be 110mm at the front and 115mm at the rear, this to be measured once the car has been filled with water and oil and with the driver on board and a full tank of fuel.

FACTORY RECOMMENDED WHEEL SETTINGS		
	Front	**Rear**
Toe-in	1–2mm	5–6mm
Camber	-10°	0°

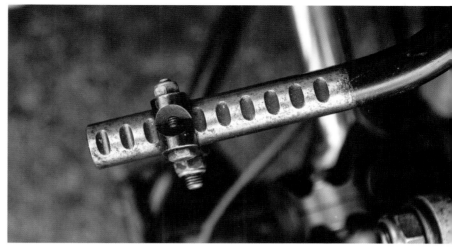

As regards ride height, Article 253 (a) required vehicles in Class A of Appendix J to be able to drive over a block or mass measuring 80 x 80cm and with a height of 10cm. This had to be achieved with the driver on board, its oil and water tanks full and with sufficient fuel to start the race. The car had to perform this test under the power of its own engine and was intended to demonstrate the ride height of the car in typical FIA legalistic fashion.

ABOVE LEFT Connected to the top of the hub (black bar from the right) is the top radius link. With this and the bottom radius link one can adjust wheelbase, toe-in and castor angle. Connected to this by means of a rose joint is the top link, which is used to adjust the camber. The large aluminium fitting in the bottom right is the brake cooling duct. The suspension set-up on each corner of the car is fully adjustable, and although it looks quite complicated it's actually relatively simple. *(Author)*

ABOVE The notched settings can be clearly seen here on the anti-roll bar. Moving its clamp towards the rear of the car will soften the anti-roll bar, while moving it towards the front will stiffen it. Moving the clamp backwards or forwards in this way has the effect of lengthening or shortening the lever effect of the anti-roll bar. *(Author)*

Brakes

The Ferrari 512 has two independent brake circuits, one for the front and one for the rear. Each is operated by its own master cylinder and can be balanced via a balance bar on the brake pedal to alter the front/rear ratio. In terms of hardware, the 512 is fitted with ventilated discs on all four wheels. Ferrari advised that the brake pad thickness should not be less than 10mm (0.39in) on the front and 9mm (0.35in) on the rear.

One front and one rear brake should be bled together, with about 1cm of free play on

RIGHT The three master cylinder reservoir tanks are located conveniently just above the pedal box, in the forward compartment. Furthest from the camera is the clutch reservoir, while the other two are brake reservoir tanks. The centre reservoir is for the rear brake circuit and the one closest to the camera is for the front brake circuit. *(Author)*

RIGHT This image shows the front disc and brake calliper. *(Author)*

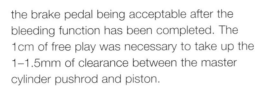

FAR RIGHT From above one can see the thickness of the front disc and pipe that delivers cool air to the back of the disc. *(Author)*

BELOW This image shows the rear disc and brake calliper. *(Author)*

BELOW RIGHT The pad quick release mechanism and the thickness of the rear disc can be seen here. *(Author)*

the brake pedal being acceptable after the bleeding function has been completed. The 1cm of free play was necessary to take up the 1–1.5mm of clearance between the master cylinder pushrod and piston.

Following an endurance race, it was advisable to check the discs for lateral runout. This is evidenced by the side-to-side movement of the brake disc as it's slowly rotated, and in the case of the 512 S should not exceed 0.05mm (0.002in). When lateral runout exceeds these limits, excessive pad and disc wear can

result, and if this exists in the front brakes vibration will be felt in the steering wheel. Vibration in the driver's seat would indicate a problem with the rear brakes.

Up front the 512 S is fitted with type 18-4/411-966 Girling callipers and Ferodo DS11-18/4 pads with a disc thickness of 32mm. On the rear it has Girling BR callipers and uses Ferodo DS11-BR pads with an 18mm disc thickness. Brake fluid replenishment should be done using Castrol Girling Amber fluid.

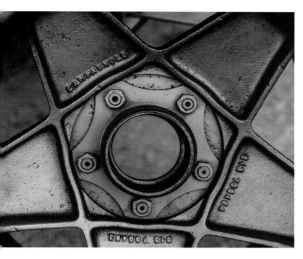

FAR LEFT
Campagnolo, well known for the manufacture of bicycle parts worldwide, made these handsome rims for the Ferrari 512. *(Author)*

LEFT The centre nut was a rather substantial 80mm across the flats. *(Author)*

BELOW LEFT The 80mm wheel-nut socket used on the Ferrari 512. *(Ten Tenths)*

BELOW The gorgeous Campagnolo wheels fitted on the Ferrari 512. *(Don Heiny, courtesy of RM Sotheby's)*

Wheels and tyres

Wheels on the Ferrari 512 were made by Campagnolo of Italy. A well-known and highly reputable manufacturer of cycling hardware, Campagnolo made wheels for a limited number of Italian high-performance road and racing cars such as Ferrari, Alfa Romeo Montreal and Lancia.

Unlike other race cars of the period that had splined hubs, the Campagnolo wheels are held in place by way of pegs. Holding the wheels in place requires a torque setting of 425ft/lb, and the centre nut holding the wheel on is a massive 80mm across the flats.

On its introduction, the Ferrari 512 was fitted with 4.75/11.50 x 15 rubber up front and 600/14.50 x 15 at the rear. While the factory cars were shod with Firestone rubber, the privateer teams would fit tyres from whatever manufacturer they were contracted to. Chinetti's NART team, Roger Penske, Jacques Swaters and David Piper, for instance, ran their 512s on Goodyear tyres.

RIGHT The interior of the 512 was a spartan environment. *(Author)*

RIGHT A simple pull-cord opened the door. *(Author)*

RIGHT The air circulation inside the cockpit could be improved by opening this simple sliding window. *(Author)*

Interior

As is typical of any top-level racing car, the cockpit isn't built for comfort but rather to ensure sufficient space for the controls necessary to carry out the task of driving the car fast. Very often the cockpit was a downright awkward environment where the driver had to sit uncomfortably while driving the projectile in which he was cocooned, at frightening speeds and sometimes for hours on end. It was required by the regulations that the car had two doors so that access to the cockpit could be gained from either side with equal ease. This was partly no doubt in case you wished to carry a theoretical passenger, but more importantly so that trackside crew could extract the driver following an accident.

The regulations didn't cater for any level of driver comfort either, as safety was their only concern. Article 292 (f) of the FIA Sporting Code stated that: 'The car shall have an adequate firewall to prevent the passage of flame from the engine compartment or from under the car into the cockpit. Openings in the firewall for the passage of engine controls, wires, and lines shall be of the minimum size necessary. The floor of the cockpit shall be constructed so as to protect the driver by preventing the entry of gravel, oil, water, and debris from the road and engine. Bottom panels or belly panels shall be adequately vented to prevent the accumulation of liquid.' Article 292 (h) ensured that 'adequate ventilation shall be provided to prevent the accumulation of fumes inside the car.'

From the outside a simple push-button opened the door, which hinged forwards and was held open by a simple spring mechanism. Access to the cockpit isn't a simple matter, but involves the driver supporting himself with one hand on the roof and the other on the aluminium sill while he thrusts his left foot in and under the steering wheel. The right foot then follows, sliding under the steering wheel and into the foot well. The foot well is a very narrow and cramped area because the wheel well encroaches on the driver's right. The centre of the car houses only the console, while the gear shift and linkages are located on the driver's right in the wide sill.

Once seated – or perhaps when lying in the car is a better way to describe the driver's position – one's knees are tight up against the underside of the steering wheel, which means that there's a lot of rubbing and scuffing as the driver wrestles with the wheel. When eventually seated, the driver's right hand falls naturally on to the gear lever and his right forearm sits

ABOVE LEFT Access to the cockpit from the outside was gained via this simple push-button door release. *(Author)*

ABOVE There was not a lot of space inside the cockpit when the driver was seated, as can be seen in this photograph with the author's knees tight up against the steering wheel. *(Author)*

comfortably on the aluminium panel covering the fuel bladder. Rearward vision is surprisingly good, as the driver has two exterior mirrors, one

LEFT The driver's seat with racing harness. *(Author)*

FAR LEFT The dashboard instruments were simple and few in number. *(Author)*

LEFT The most prominent instrument in the 512 was the large rev counter, in this case red-lined at 7,600rpm. *(Author)*

RIGHT Over the years many different owners have 'personalised' their 512s to suit their needs or driving style. *(Author)*

ABOVE There are two fire extinguisher system buttons, one on the dashboard for the driver to operate and a second on the outside for track officials to access in the event of driver injury. The switch marked 'LPR' is to turn on the four Facet Red Top lift pumps that draw fuel up into the collector tank. To the right is a toggle switch marked 'HP', which is for the high-pressure fuel pump that feeds fuel from the collector tank to the injector pump at 11kg/cm^2 pressure. This is switched on when starting the engine. Once the engine is running the HP switch is turned off, because a belt-driven mechanical fuel pump that runs off the crankshaft then takes over, feeding the injectors at the same pressure level. The black push-button on the top right is the all-important 'Start' button. *(Author)*

RIGHT By racing car standards the space in the foot well is quite generous, but it's still cramped in that it causes one's legs to get jammed up underneath the steering wheel. David Hobbs complained that his right foot would lose feeling after 20 minutes. *(Author)*

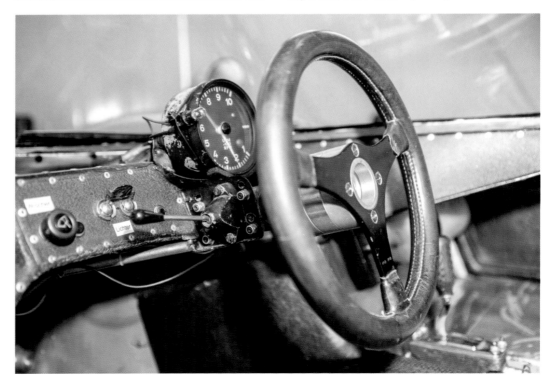

RIGHT A naked bulb taped to the outside of the rev counter is all that illuminates the main instrument for this driver. *(Author)*

mounted on the top of each fender, as well as the roof-mounted mirror. Contrary to expectations, this roof mirror provides a very good view over the top of the airbox and rear wings.

Controls were kept to an absolute minimum, and the dashboard is both plain and basic, as would be expected. Over the years, and in the hands of different owners, the dials and switches may have had their positions swapped on the dashboard, but basically all the same switchgear was retained on the cars viewed during the research for this book. This included: ammeter, fuel/pressure gauge, oil pressure gauge, direction indicator light, ammeter warning light, electric pumps warning light, electric fuel pump switch, night illumination numbers switch, horn button, instrument light resistor, spot-light switch, water/oil temperature combination gauge, wiper switch/screen squirter, dip switch lever, direction indicator switch and ignition switch. Taking centre stage is a large Veglia rev counter marked rather ambitiously to 12,000rpm and framed rather appropriately by a Momo steering wheel.

Stretching across the cockpit from left to right and passing under the driver's knees is a sizeable tunnel that houses the fuel pipe connecting the left and right tanks. In accordance with the regulations governing Group 5 cars, the 512 had to be fitted with a passenger seat, although such a passenger would have had to be of very slight stature!

Fuel tanks

The FIA regulations stipulated in Article 253 (j) that the fuel tank capacity of the class in which the Ferrari 512 raced should have a total capacity not exceeding 140 litres. In 1969 the

RIGHT Ferrari 512 M fuel quick-filler cap. *(Author)*

RIGHT With the front bodywork removed, the fuel filler neck is revealed. *(Author)*

FAR RIGHT The Ferrari 512 could be refuelled from either side depending on which side the refuelling rig was. *(Author)*

BELOW The covered 'hump' that passed under the driver's knees housed the pipe that connected the two fuel tanks. *(Author)*

authorities were keen to embrace new safety technology as regards fuel tanks, and they encouraged manufacturers of cars in Group 4 (later Group 5) to fit fuel 'bladders'.

Article 292 (g) specified 'that no part of any fuel, oil or water tank shall be exposed to any part of the driver and passenger compartment. Fuel tanks shall be vented to prevent the accumulation of fumes and to prevent fumes from passing into the driver or engine compartment. Fuel tanks shall be isolated by means of bulkheads so that in the case of spillage, leakage or a failure of the tank, the fuel will not pass into the driver or engine compartment or around any part of the exhaust system.'

Carried within the sills of the 512 chassis were two fuel bladders totalling 120 litres, plus a reserve tank of 6.5 litres. Woody Woodard recalled, 'There were two bladders, one left-side and one right-side. The one on the left side was slightly larger because the shift linkage was located on the right, down inside the sill compartment where the bladder was. Combined they held about 32 gallons [120 litres]. My guess is the left-side was probably 17 gallons [64 litres] and the right-side was probably 15 gallons [56 litres].'

The Ferrari 512 can be refuelled from either side, as the two tanks are connected by means of a tube that passes beneath the driver's knees. The overflow from the fuel distributor is directed to a small reserve fuel tank (6.5 litres or 1¾ gallons) via a pressure limiting valve, whence it is returned to the main tanks. Should the driver find himself with both main tanks empty he can call on the 6.5-litre reserve tank, the fuel from which is fed directly to the high-pressure pumps.

Each fuel tank is fitted with an electric fuel

LEFT The 512 S had a single large headlamp faired into the front wing, but this car is using a non-original Lucas lamp. *(Author)*

pump, either a Conelec or a Carter unit. The fuel passes through a Fram filter into a reservoir, which is also fitted with a filter. The reservoir is further fitted with a de-aeration system for the removal of oxygen from the fuel. Fuel from the reservoir is fed to the Lucas Mk II high-pressure pumps (fuel pressure should be at $11kg/cm^2$ or $155lb/in^2$) which in turn feed the fuel distributor. The fuel is delivered to the cylinders in the following order: 1-2-3-4-5-6-7-8-9-10-11-12, and doesn't follow the engine's cylinder firing order.

LEFT This 512 M is fitted with the correct original Marchal lamp. *(Riiko Nüüd)*

BELOW On the 512 S a pair of Carello driving lights were mounted next to each other in the centre of the nose. The 512 M did not have these. *(Author)*

Lamps and lighting

The Ferrari 512 S and 512 M are both equipped with two headlamps that satisfied the FIA regulations. These consist of a single Marchal headlamp on each side, with a small parking light mounted in the floor of the headlamp binnacle.

'Ferrari at the time had a contract with Marchal, so the big headlight was a Marchal,' François Sicard explained. One might therefore expect that the tail lamps would be by the same manufacturer, but this isn't the case. 'Those were Carello lights,' Sicard added with a smile, 'I remember they came from a truck!' The light

RIGHT Sticker on the rear of the lamp unit showing the correct reference number and settings. *(Riiko Nüüd)*

FAR RIGHT The 512's rear lamps were manufactured by Carello. *(Riiko Nüüd)*

RIGHT Mandatory exterior battery cut-out switch. *(Author)*

BELOW The fuse box and electrical connector board was located inside the passenger door aperture. *(Author)*

housing at the rear, on both S and M models, consists of individual brake lights and indicator roundels, separated by a rectangular reflector.

It was, of course, in the best interests of the driver to have the best lights possible in order to make night-driving easier and safer, but as with all things in motor sport, there was always the fight with unnecessary weight.

Electrical

It was compulsory for a closed race car to be fitted with two general circuit breakers, one internally for activation by the driver and one externally, clearly marked for activation by marshals should it be necessary.

The electrical system is based on a 12V negative earth system. The lightweight battery in the 512 S is located as low as possible in the front compartment where the wiper motor sits, along with all the piping for the oil radiators. On the 512 M the battery was relocated and mounted on the left-hand side aluminium sill

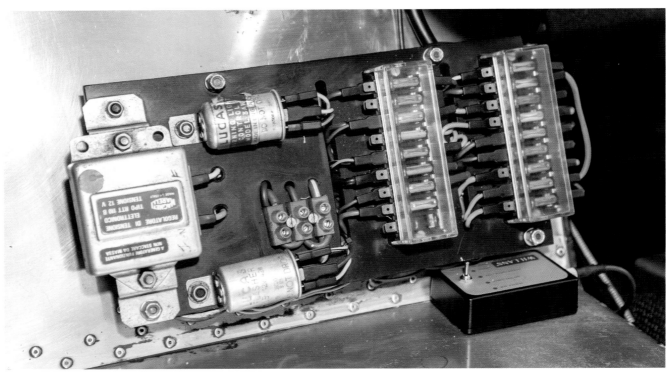

ABOVE The Ferrari 512 S (in this instance chassis 1026) is fitted with a Willans electrically operated fire extinguisher system. This can be activated by either the driver by means of a fire button on the dashboard or by a track marshal from the exterior of the car. *(Author)*

next to the fuse box. One of the benefits of this was to bring as much weight as possible to a position within the wheelbase, thereby improving the car's weight distribution as Mauro Forghieri explained earlier. The battery had to be fully enclosed.

Chapter Three

The engineer's view

Much was expected of the new Ferrari 512 S when it was introduced, and in all honesty it should have delivered more than it did. The 512 had the makings of yet another legendary sports racer from Maranello, and many of those who worked on it in period, as well as the loyal *Tifosi*, forgave it for underachieving because it just looked so good.

'It was a pretty standard engine, gearbox and suspension configuration. The only thing fairly new for us was the mechanical fuel injection which replaced the carburettors.'

— Dick Fritz, NART team manager

OPPOSITE Nick Mason's 512 S, chassis 1026, with nose removed. *(Author)*

ABOVE First raced as a works car at the 1970 Le Mans 24-Hours in 512 S spec, chassis 1034 was almost completely destroyed in that race. It was rebuilt in the 1990s to 512 M specification. (RM Sotheby's)

BELOW Disappointingly Dan Gurney and Chuck Parsons lasted only 464 laps in the 1970 Daytona 24-Hours in the #25 Chinetti NART car (chassis 1014), retiring with gearbox trouble. (LAT)

Running a Ferrari 512 S and 512 M in period

'In the beginning the factory would send different engineers to different races,' said Mauro Forghieri, 'sometimes Gianni Marelli, Giacomo Caliri or Giancarlo Bussi.' Forghieri would himself attend races when the 512 was still new, but as 1970 rolled into 1971 and Ferrari withdrew its support for the car, it was Gaetano Florini, manager of the Modena service department, who was responsible for the customers. As this was Florini's function, it stood to reason that he would be seen at the track supporting the factory's customers.

North American Racing Team (NART)

One such private race team was that run by Luigi Chinetti (1901–94), a man as large as life itself. Chinetti entered the Le Mans 24-Hour race no less than 12 times, and won it on three occasions (1932 and 1934 for Alfa Romeo, and in 1949 for Ferrari). It was Chinetti who, together with Lord Selsdon, in 1949 gave Ferrari its first win in the 17th running of the legendary French race driving a Ferrari 166MM. Chinetti would drive all but 30 minutes of the 24-hour race that year, an astonishing feat.

That victory no doubt helped Chinetti in his

bid to open the first Ferrari dealership in North America later that year, a relationship with the factory that lasted some 30 years, firmly establishing the brand in North America. A decade later, in 1958, Luigi Chinetti established the North American Racing Team (NART), in an attempt to draw customers to the Ferrari brand through its racing victories.

At the time the 512 was launched Dick Fritz was team manager of Luigi Chinetti's NART team. 'When a new race car came out, if there were enough of them then we'd usually buy one,' Dick Fritz explained, 'but if there weren't enough then we'd usually end up getting it the next year. Fortunately, with the 512s in 1970 there were enough to go around.' The reason, of course, that there were enough 512s to go around was because Ferrari had to build 25 cars, and desperately needed private teams to race them. 'I had six cars in my team that year,' recalled Fritz. 'There was the 512 S, two 312Ps, one Daytona, a 275 GTBC and a 275 LM. I think we paid $20,000 for the 512 S, and that was without a roll bar or seat belts and with no fuel pump.'

So what was the 512 S like to work on? Without exception, those who worked on the Ferrari 512 in period all agreed that the race car was 'pretty straightforward and uncomplicated', especially when compared with the Porsche 917. For the Chinetti mechanics, running a Ferrari dealership and workshop would have given them the opportunity to familiarise themselves with the mechanicals. Fritz again: 'It was a pretty standard engine, gearbox and suspension configuration. The only thing fairly new for us was the mechanical fuel injection which replaced the carburettors.' In time the fuel injection proved quite straightforward to manage, as setting it for the different mixtures required at various circuits was adjusted by means of a notched cam.

Dick Fritz remembered when their first 512 S arrived in 1970: 'The 512 S arrived at Daytona, and we did the practice and qualifying but we had a lot of problems, as did the factory cars, because the cross-member holding the back suspension had a lot of cracks in it. That was because it had never raced, and to build 25 cars and get them homologated wasn't easy, which meant that the factory didn't have enough time to test the car. So we welded on a reinforcement, and that fixed it. The engine was working well but we had a lot of problems with the oil tank on the banking, because we lost oil. We had too much brake on the front but there's

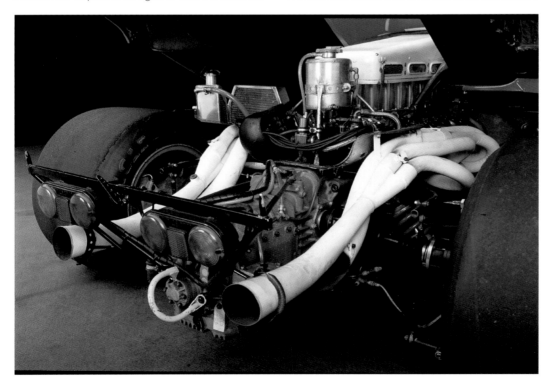

an adjustment on the pedals to eliminate the
problem; so we had to adjust the pressure on
the brakes, but that's quite normal.'
Following a big race, such as the Daytona
24-Hours, chief mechanic Nereo Iori and team
mechanic François Sicard would take the car
apart and check everything ready for the next
race. Sicard explained why: 'If you don't do that
after 40 hours on the 512, you're sure to have a
blow-up. And that's what happened to me with
a 512 S we bought for Gregg Young that had
raced at Le Mans. At Sebring, Masten Gregory
was driving that car and he placed it in third on
the grid, and he said, "You know, that engine is
very loose." I said, "What do you mean?" And
he said, "That car has got a lot of miles on it
because it's very fast, and you know, when the
engine is new it isn't like this." And he was right,
because after three or four hours the engine blew.

'We had a bar to align the crankshaft, and
we also put in new valves, new bearings and
sometimes we'd replace the pistons too. We
also had to check the crankshaft. We had
another case, where we'd done one race, and
Chinetti decided to run the car in the Salt Flats
speed trials in 1974, and Nereo Iori said we had
to do the engine again. But Chinetti didn't want
to do it. At Le Mans there are a lot of turns
and this allows the engine to breathe better
because it isn't running at 7,000rpm all the time
like it was on the Salt Flats. I remember he said
his foot was always down on the accelerator,
and we blew the engine because that engine
had a lot of hours on it.' This car was chassis
number 1020, and was driven to a world speed
record by none other than Luigi Chinetti Jr, Paul
Newman, Graham Hill and Milt Minter.

François Sicard recalled the first 512 that
came into Chinetti's workshop. 'We didn't have
a dyno – the engine was done in the factory
the first time and they tested it on the dyno, but
they never gave us the test results. Actually they
never gave away anything, so we never really
knew. We asked Forghieri the same thing, and
he said, "Maybe 545bhp," but we did a lot of
polishing of engine parts.'

Asked if the 512 had a weak point, Fritz shot
back without hesitation, 'Yes, its aerodynamics. It
just wasn't nearly as aerodynamic as a Porsche
917, no way, not even the 512 M. If you looked
at the speed differential between the 917 and
the 512 on the Mulsanne Straight, there was
probably a 10mph difference in top speed. The
917 had a much smoother airflow over the body,
and the Ferrari was much more angular.

'I remember Sam Posey coming in and
telling me at Le Mans in 1971, "Dick, the
Porsches are going by me on the Mulsanne
Straight. You can't believe it, but they just pull
away." The 512 was heavier and the handling
wasn't as good. It wasn't horrible, but it wasn't
as good as the Porsche. I remember Brian
Redman telling me up at Watkins Glen, he said,
"Dick, if this car, chassis and suspension wasn't
like a truck, this would be an incredible car as
far as the engine and power is concerned."'

Fritz described Nereo Iori as a great
mechanic who'd been at the Ferrari factory 'and
then came over to work for us at Chinetti, and
ended up staying in America. He was great with

engines and with gearboxes too. I remember one time I worked with Iori at Watkins Glen, and we balanced the engine very carefully and also got some new valve springs from a customer who had a company in Connecticut called Associated Spring. We'd told him that we were having problems with the valve springs at around 8,600rpm and he gave us some springs that enabled us to run the engine at 9,000rpm, that's why we had the fastest 512. If you compare it to Roger Penske's, I think we were running at 183mph at the end of the main straight and he was running at 180mph, and we could do this because we used different gearing and ran to a higher rpm.'

Although the gearbox was a good unit, some teams and drivers did experience problems with the gear shift and linkages. The Chinetti team would adjust the linkages before practice

and then again after practice, and in this way it shifted gears correctly, but in order to avoid problems it required this kind of attention regularly. The gear lever itself, however, broke off in Dan Gurney's hand once, and in Fritz's opinion it was a bad design. It was rectangular in cross-section and came up to a point where it was flat, and right at that point is where the shift mount screwed on, creating a stress riser, which is a point where forces can concentrate the load and break it.

François Sicard, the Chinetti team mechanic recalled, 'Dan Gurney raced our first 512 at Daytona in 1970, and he broke the shift linkage. The piece of wood that they used as a gear knob was very high on the shift lever, and where it was screwed in was very thin, and he broke it. Gurney was big and his glove was broad, and every time he changed gears he'd grind his

ABOVE This Ferrari 512 S (chassis 1006) was delivered to Luigi Chinetti's NART in 1970.
(Don Heiny, courtesy of RM Sotheby's)

'Within each race there might be different rpm limits set at different times in the race, and we used to do that. In general, if it was a 24-hour race we'd use a lower rpm. So, for example, we'd probably pick 8,400rpm, but at some point in the race we might go down to 8,200 because we had a large enough lead over the car behind us. The object always, for us at NART, was to finish the race, because you never knew what would happen in the last 20 minutes. So we'd often change the limit based on what position we were in, and how many hours into the race we'd progressed. We never blew an engine in any of the endurance races where we ran the 512. Other things could go wrong – the fuel injection was pretty archaic and metals weren't as strong, but you know, it was very different 40 years ago.

'Where we'd allow the rpm to go up would be at the end of the main straight where the car was slowly building up speed and maybe we could utilise that extra 200 or 300rpm to complete that section at the highest possible speed. We often did that, as this approach would also take a lot less out of the engine, but that would be discussed beforehand.

'At Daytona, for example, we were running

RIGHT The Chinetti cars wore the NART badge with pride. This is a 1970 Ferrari 512 S (chassis 1006).
(Don Heiny, courtesy of RM Sotheby's)

first when the Porsche 917 that Pedro Rodríguez was driving suffered a broken gearbox. We, on the other hand, had one bent valve, which I'm guessing was the result of one of the drivers over-revving the engine a good bit, so we were running on 11 cylinders. In such a case you don't stress the engine, so we could probably only get around 7,800rpm. Although we had a pretty good lead the car wasn't running perfectly, but once the Porsche gearbox was repaired Pedro went out and caught up to us and beat us by about half a lap after 24 hours of racing. So you can't pin down exactly one particular rev limit for one race, because it changes.

'When we got some new inner and outer valve springs in 1971 we set the car up at Watkins Glen so we could max out at the end of the straightaway at close to 9,000rpm, but that was the only time we did that. I had got some different gears from Roger Penske once that I collected from his shop in town. The gears were all tied together with cord in a wooden box from the factory, and there was a tag on each one that gave the ratios. When we ran at Watkins Glen using 9,000rpm at the end of the main straight, we were about 2 to 3mph faster than Roger's car at that point. I told Roger that the reason was because Iori and I had spent a whole Sunday balancing that engine very carefully before putting it together, so that we could run a higher rpm, but I think I forgot to tell him about the valve springs.

'In shorter races, let's say a six-hour race like Watkins Glen for example, we'd more likely use 8,600rpm, because that was about all we could get out of the engine with the valve springs that were delivered from the factory. We might set a certain rpm limit that we'd use for most of the race and then, as it got near the end, we might change based on the position of the car, and the position of the car behind us. When we finished third at Le Mans, for instance, we had to try to save the car because a lot of things were broken.'

Asked if they would run with different rev limits in qualifying versus the race, Fritz replied, 'No, we didn't, the reason being that when we put the car together we'd try to run it in the race just as we'd run it in practice so that we didn't mess anything up. It was a rule we tried to follow, that we wouldn't mess with it once it had gone through practice and it was running okay and everything else was fine. All you'd do at that point was to check everything, so we generally wouldn't change a thing. Also, we didn't change the gear ratios for qualifying.

'In addition, as Luigi Chinetti senior and I saw it, qualifying back then was never that important because usually, in a 24-hour race, the cars finished a good bit apart. So if, for instance, you qualified fifth instead of first, it meant that you might be 300ft behind the pole car, so it didn't mean that much. There was no sense in running the guts out of the engine just to qualify first, simply to be at the front, when in fact you might hurt the engine in trying to do it.

'Today, though, everything is different. Cars generally don't have mechanical failures in long-distance races any more. Look at Audi and what they've done – their cars just start and it's a sprint right to the end. It was certainly different back then. Reliability was different – the amount of testing that was done, the amount of money spent on everything, was also very different. When you consider the 512s and the 917s, neither company was large

– in fact they were quite small, so there was less testing and maybe even no aerodynamic testing. Once the car was designed you'd just hope that it was aerodynamically sound and you'd have to work on it later to improve it if it wasn't good in the beginning. That doesn't happen any more.'

ABOVE Sam Posey and Ronnie Bucknum drove the #11 NART Ferrari 512 S (chassis 1014) to a fine fourth-place finish in the 1970 Le Mans. *(LAT)*

BELOW Roberto Giordanelli prepares to test NART 512 S chassis 1006 back in 2000. The car is still wearing #23 from its second-place finish in the 1971 Daytona 24-Hours. *(Peter Collins)*

glove against the body, and as the shifter was very small it was very hard to move through the gears, but he managed.'

Sicard reported no problems with the 512's gearbox from a maintenance point of view, at a time when the Porsche 917 experienced many gearbox problems in competition. He recalled: 'On the 512 S we had a little problem with the gears and the ring and pinion because it was a bit short, but the gearbox on the 512 M was different – the ring and pinion was bigger. But we never had any problems with the gearbox itself. We just changed the bearings and that was it. With the clutch it was the same thing, the clutch was very good.'

In the 1971 Daytona race, the two drivers in the #20 Chinetti 512 M, chassis 1014, were Gregg Young and Masten Gregory. Unfortunately the car retired after just 16 laps with engine trouble. However, the interesting thing here is the willingness of teams to help each other. François Sicard picked up the story: 'Penske was the only one who'd done a lot of testing at Daytona, and he had a lot of problems with the oil tank early on. I talked to him about this, and he gave me one of their tanks which I put on the car, and that's when Masten Gregory put the car in fifth place on the grid because everybody else had a problem with their oil. Penske told me that he'd had a lot of problems with the oil and so they'd made a new tank, and it's one of these that he gave me. It's still on the car today!'

When asked who his best 512 driver was, Fritz considered his response for a few moments. 'If you look at all of the drivers NART ever had, we had Gurney and Mario Andretti, Stirling Moss and Pedro Rodríguez – I mean, I could just go on and on. But who was the best in a 512? I'd probably have to say Sam Posey, because he would persevere and finish the race, and in an endurance race you really do need to finish. The problem is that you can be faster, but break the car and not finish. Tony Adamowicz was an equal with Posey, but obviously Dan Gurney was a spectacular driver. But we beat Roger Penske in every race in which we participated!'

The 512 M had more power than the S – in fact output jumped from 550bhp to around 620bhp, an increase of more than %10 – but where did this increase come from? 'The engine was redone. It had new pistons and new sleeves, the cam was more aggressive and the valves were a bit bigger,' Sicard explained. The chassis of the 512 M was the same as the 512 S, but the M was lighter than the S, which had a lot of heavy fibreglass body panels.

Penske Racing Team

John 'Woody' Woodard started working for Penske Racing on 14 January 1969, and in that first year he was chief mechanic on Mark Donohue's SCCA Trans-Am Championship-winning Camaro. The following season was Penske's first with the AMC Javelin, in which Donohue took three victories, finishing second in the championship that year to Parnelli Jones. Right after the final Trans-Am race of 1970 at Riverside, Woodard was called into Roger Penske's office and told that instead of running two cars in the Trans-Am Championship in 1971, they would run just one.

'But they also planned to run a Ferrari in the World Manufacturers Championship,' Woodard recalled, 'and by the way it would be arriving from California any day, so that was my job for the winter.' The car, a Ferrari 512 S with chassis number 1040, was originally sold new to Chris Cord and Steve Earle, and driven by Jim Adams in various Can-Am events in 1970. In order to get some idea of what they had bought and its performance potential, Woodard and the Penske team took the car over to Summit Point in West Virginia to get some baseline tests done. Mark Donohue was to be the driver, and it was planned to run the car in four long-distance events – Daytona, Sebring, Le Mans and Watkins Glen. By this time talks had already begun with David Hobbs, who was to partner Donohue in this campaign.

Chassis 1040 had been raced on only a few occasions in the Can-Am series by Jim Adams, and the car came directly to Penske with no spare parts, just a couple of extra wheels.

Unfortunately it rained for three days at Summit Point, so after the 'failed' tests it was decided that the car would be completely torn down to the bare frame, which Woodard started on immediately. 'Back then,' he explained, 'the Ferrari frame consisted of a steel tube spaceframe with soft aluminium panels riveted

on in areas like the firewall and floor. The soft aluminium, though, wasn't any good for that purpose, so we literally removed every rivet and every piece of aluminium. Penske then rented a fabricator by the name of Lujie Lesovsky from Holman & Moody. He was an elderly guy well into his 60s by then, but he was probably one of the world's premier fabricators. When it came to bending metal, welding or forming, Lesovsky was a magician.'

When Penske took delivery of chassis 1040 it was still in 512 S open-top form, and as they wanted it converted to M-spec it was Lesovsky's job to fabricate the aluminium firewall and lightweight roof by hand. Cox recalled that 'Roger contracted Berry Plastics to build a new body and he ordered two noses and one tail, so we had a spare nose.' Berry Plastics, also based in Southern California, fabricated the fibreglass body parts for the Penske Ferrari. According to Kirk White, they weighed about half as much as the factory bodies.

One thing that the team learned at the rained-out Summit Point test was the oil scavenge system was a very poor design, which resulted in Woodard completely reworking the plumbing. He also built a new-design dry sump tank. The factory wiring harness too was 'absolutely horrible', so he gutted the wiring and installed all-new gauges, switches and lights. 'I made up my own harness and that harness is still on that car today,' he added proudly. Although the wiring harness was completely rebuilt and the ancillaries replaced, the Magneti Marelli ignition system was retained.

Penske developed and installed a dry break refuelling system in the 512 M, the first such system in a sports car at the time. The aviation-type dry break system had a mechanical connection for both the supply and the vent at the back of the tank, eliminating the chance of a fuel spillage. 'We were the first ones to do that, and when we arrived at Daytona with a tall fuel rig and dry break refuelling Porsche and Ferrari had never seen anything like it,' Woodard remembered.

The Penske team's 12ft-high fuel rig was a measure designed to reduce refuelling time. They first employed it in the Trans-Am Championship in 1969. In addition they had

an extender that would push the top of the rig up to 24ft. This system was developed and built by Sun Oil, Sunoco being Penske's well-known sponsor. Unfortunately, the 24ft refuelling system was soon outlawed by the Trans-Am authorities, but the 12ft version remained legal. Penske used this rig at Daytona and Sebring, but at Le Mans they had to use the refuelling equipment provided by the circuit. The last race for the Penske 512 M was run at Watkins Glen, where they used the 24ft tower. 'Our first pit stop in the six-hour race was for fuel only and it took 2.4 seconds to refuel!' remembered Woodard. 'People were just shaking their heads – they couldn't believe it! Twenty-four feet high is a lot of head pressure.'

The first thing that chief engineer Don Cox did was to give the Penske Ferrari more downforce. 'We made our own rear wings,' said Woodard. 'We had a small rear wing for Daytona and Le Mans, and then we had a pretty good-sized rear wing for Sebring and Watkins Glen. Don Cox designed the full-width rear wings, and Lujie Lesovsky fabricated them.'

When it came to changing the brake pads during a race, Penske's brake puck retractor system attracted a lot of attention. Woodard explained: 'What this consisted of was a dry brake fitting that literally sat on top of the master cylinder. In the pits we had a vacuum tank and a vacuum pump that would pull a vacuum down on this tank. So when the car came into the pits, we'd attach this quick-connect fitting and by the time the car was up in the air and the

ABOVE The #6 Penske/Sunoco Ferrari 512 M (chassis 1040) gives it all in the 1971 Sebring 12-Hours before being hit by Rodríguez in the fourth hour. (LAT)

wheels were off the brake pucks had retracted completely and the brake pads would literally fall out. We were doing brake pad changes in less than a minute, and Porsche was taking three or four minutes. I met Mauro Forghieri at Le Mans – in fact he searched me out, to enquire about our brake pad retraction system.'

Woody Woodard and his team also had systems built into the car for pressurised oil and water refilling. This meant that if the car lost water for some reason, or if additional oil was required, the team could simply connect up the pressurised bottles and the job would be done in seconds. The fuel pickup system that Ferrari designed was almost completely ineffectual, according to Woodard. 'It just sloshed around in the bladders, and hopefully it got to the pickup. We designed an all-new pickup system where we could get almost every drop out of the fuel bladders.'

Italian car design and aluminium craftsmanship has long been admired, so much so that many regarded Italy as the capital of the world in this field. So it came as a bit of a surprise when Woody Woodard commented, 'The quality of Ferrari's aluminium castings and their machining was outstanding, but their fabrication quality was very poor.' Regarding the reputation of the Italian craftsmanship, he said, 'Well, it didn't show on this car compared to what was coming out of England at the time.'

When designing and developing a race car, there will always be some component that's awkwardly positioned or difficult to get at. In this respect the 512 was no exception, because the mechanical fuel pump that provides fuel to the injection system is located below the front of the crankshaft, where it picks up a lot of dirt. 'Not only was the design and location of the pump a weak link, but it was driven by a tiny half-inch wide gilmer belt, and this created a number of problems. We had to stop and change it twice during the Daytona 24-Hours,' Woodard revealed.

Penske had all of his engines prepared by Traco, an engine specialist based in Los Angeles, California, which was right across the country from the Penske workshops. Woodard explained why they followed this routine: 'Traco didn't want to get into doing a Ferrari engine, but we kind of forced them into doing it because we wouldn't trust anybody else. We went to Daytona with both the new engine and the old engine as a spare. After that race it went back to Traco and they tore it down and rebuilt it, but they could never get the heads to seal again properly. We wound up using the original old engine at Sebring that Traco had rebuilt a couple of times, and we went to Le Mans with that same engine too.'

Mark Donohue's racing accomplishments are well known. He was undoubtedly a formidable racer, and like many other top drivers he had his personal likes and dislikes. One of his dislikes was differentials – he wanted what's known as a spool or a locker, where both wheels would spin at exactly the same time so that they don't differentiate. According to Woody Woodard every car in which Donohue was successful after Daytona, even the later 917s, was fitted with a spool which completely locked up the differential. Woodard expanded, 'We designed and had built a lock differential for Sebring that made the car a lot quicker, but David Hobbs always had trouble driving it. Mark's theory was that he didn't want a drive wheel to *not* pull, he wanted both wheels pulling all the time, and he changed his driving style to be able to drive it the way that he wanted to drive it. We didn't run the locker at Le Mans because there you don't really have any corners like you had at other circuits.'

On the suspension, Woody Woodard recalled that they did a minor relocation of a swingarm to change the swingarm length of the rear suspension. Donohue also wanted to do the front suspension because he felt the swingarm was too short, but to extend it required major surgery and it was just something that the team never got around to doing. 'We did modify the suspension to take heavier sway bars, because we had quite an inventory of different sway bars with splined ends so we could very quickly change one. We had quite a spring selection too, and fortunately Don Cox found a company to make a range that fitted that car, because you need quite an array of springs to take a car on the banking at Daytona and then on the road surface at Sebring.'

David Hobbs, driving partner of Mark Donohue in the Penske Ferrari, said, 'It's probably one of the best-known Ferraris in the world. It's certainly the best-known 512. And it never won anything!' Kirk White recalled the first time the car was revealed at Daytona: 'We had our test weekend at Daytona in January 1971, and actually it was the first time that several of us had seen the car in its completed form. When it came out of the ramp truck I was standing with Bloys Britt, who at the time was the chief motor sports writer for the *New York Times*. He was like Alfred Neubauer, you could hardly get a smile out of him, and Bloys just quietly said to me, "That is the single most beautiful racing car I have ever seen."'

Don Cox went to work for Roger Penske in November 1969, and his initial job was as engineer on the Trans-Am Javelin. At the end of the 1969 season Penske left Chevrolet, having decided to run a Javelin the following year in the Trans-Am series. This was because essentially GM didn't offer any financial aid, and as American Motors was willing to do that the swap was an easy decision. Cox did the 1970 season with the Penske Javelin, which brought Donohue a second place that season, and, as Cox added humbly, 'Somewhere along the way I became chief engineer. But chief engineer doesn't mean much when you're the only one.'

Cox admitted that he had never heard of the 512 until he saw one up in Penske's workshop one evening late in 1970. 'I'd finished up on the Javelin project, and one evening Roger called me from the office building to come up to the workshop. So I went up there and the Ferrari was just sitting there in a bay, still in its factory red colour. At that time we were running Javelins, Indy, Formula 5000, USAC, I can't even remember all the different things we were involved in. Kirk White was there with Roger and Mark, and they were all just standing around. Roger announced to me at that point that they were going to run the Ferrari in the long-distance races at Daytona and Sebring. He was well known for doing that sort of thing – all of a sudden a new car would appear and Roger would tell us that we were going to race in a new series. And so we'd all endeavour to make it happen.'

Penske was watching Cox in order to gauge his reaction to the car, and after a short while asked him what he'd do to the car to make it faster. Cox had only left Chevrolet a year or so earlier, where he'd been in R&D, being part of the team responsible for putting the wings on the Chaparrals. Assessing the newcomer in

front of him, Cox asked politely if that was the whole car, or if some additional body panels or components came with it. When Penske affirmed that it was, Cox replied, '"The first thing we should do is to put a wing on it," and Roger agreed with that, and so we came up with a wing profile that we thought would be appropriate. Once you've decided what you wanted the wing to look like, making it wasn't all that hard to do.'

Cox went on to explain that all cars have lift – all one has to do is to get them going fast enough and they'll lift off the ground. At that point what the driver would feel was a complete detachment of any input relative to the road, because with the tyres not having any load on them they can't work for you.

The cars back in 1967 and 1968 had 300–400lb/in^2 springs, and when Cox and his team first put a wing on the Chaparral, at speed, it pushed the car right down against the bump stops. 'We realised early on that we didn't want to put the load into the basic chassis, we wanted to put it directly into the uprights so that the wing forces were pushing on the tyres, and not using up all the bump travel by pushing on the car. So we mounted the wings on struts so that the wing loads went into the rear uprights. But you couldn't get too fancy with mounting the wing on the Ferrari. It had to be mounted on the body or attached to the body – it couldn't have struts as we'd had on the Chaparral

BELOW The immaculately turned-out #11 Penske Sunoco Ferrari 512 M (chassis 1040), driven by Mark Donohue and David Hobbs, was forced to retire from the 1971 Le Mans 24-Hours with a blown engine. *(LAT)*

ABOVE Works Ferrari chassis 1034 was almost completely destroyed at Le Mans in 1970. The factory salvaged what components it could and wrote off the chassis. It was only in the 1990s that the car was resurrected by a privateer to 512 M specification.
(RM Sotheby's)

because by that time they were banned.'

With the full-width wing mounted, the 512 really was more competitive, with Mark Donohue securing pole at both Daytona and Sebring in 1971. 'After we built the wing and put it on the car, I wasn't involved with it much after that, because Woody was the chief mechanic and Mark was a very capable driver and tester with engineering and technical expertise of his own. I think at least part of the reason that the car was so good was because we had a proper wing on it and we had the suspension and handling all sorted to take into account the effects of having the wing. We messed about with roll bars and springs to get it behaving in a civilised manner. And because we beat the Porsches in qualifying, we gained some credibility with them which eventually led us to the 917/30 Can-Am project.'

The task of designing and fabricating the rear wing wouldn't have taken that long, because the Penske workshop wasn't a large one, and with so many different projects going on at once Cox didn't have the luxury of time on his side. Once that step in the task was complete he'd hand it on to the next person in the chain and move on to the next project. Cox reminisced with some humour, 'Back in 1971 and 1972 we used to do around 50 races per season and we only had about ten guys on the team, but today if you do ten races a year you may

have 50 guys. When I got into motor racing I was young, maybe in my 20s, and being an engineer at a major automotive company [GM], the whole racing thing was just something that people did in their spare time – it wasn't really a profession as such. As far as I know, I was the first engineer that Penske ever employed, if you don't count Mark, because he was employed as a race car driver. But I didn't really see motor racing as having a big professional future.'

The engines that Penske had run prior to taking on the Ferrari 512 were done by Traco in California, the same outfit that did their Javelin and Chevy engines. 'They didn't know a Ferrari engine from a bushel of grapefruit,' Cox quipped, 'but they took it apart, looked it over and did whatever they could to make it run better.' At Le Mans in 1971 Mark Donohue qualified the Ferrari in fourth place behind two John Wyer works Porsche 917s and the Martini 917. Powered by the Traco-prepared engine, this was an incredibly good qualifying result for a private entry up against the might of Stuttgart. Don Cox recalled: 'At Le Mans we qualified fourth, but Ferrari insisted that in the race we run a factory engine that they'd prepped, instead of the engine Traco had built. Unfortunately their factory engine failed in the race!'

With Penske located in Philadelphia, Pennsylvania, why did he choose to send his

ABOVE Nick Mason's
512 S stretches the
legs of chassis 1026
at a very wet
Silverstone in the
1990s. *(Peter Collins)*

engines right across the country to Southern California to be prepared? The answer lay in the fact that the hot-rod movement had its origins in that part of the country, and this was the performance car scene in which Traco established its reputation. 'Traco Engineering in California was building Roger's Chevrolet Trans-Am engines,' Kirk White explained, 'and that was the most competitive racing series in America at the time. I knew that there was a lot of Southern California engineering pumped into his race cars, and Traco's engines were bullet-proof; they were great. So, part of the deal that Penske and I did – and it was just a verbal understanding – was that I said to him that I felt the Ferrari 512 was a good basic car, but if the Southern California engineers could get hold of that engine and finish it up the right way it would be a world-beater. Frankly, they found the Ferrari product to be quite good, but they did a better job of balancing it. They made some changes, but by and large the factory engines were good.'

After the Sebring win of 1970, the future must have looked bright for the 512 S. That this didn't turn out to be true is well recorded, but what was the 512's principal reason for not achieving a better record of wins? 'Insufficient development,' was Mauro Forghieri's view. 'We had to do too much to increase the power output. In those days Ferrari wasn't the

company that it is today, nor did it have the necessary resources.'

Surely Ferrari must have realised that the 512s would not stand much chance in the hands of privateers against the works Porsches, so what was Ferrari's reason for withdrawing support for the 512 in 1971? A passionate Mauro Forghieri replied, 'I was very upset, but it was necessary to move to a new, smaller sports car, and of course the decision was also based on some economical issues.'

Asked how Ferrari viewed the two-year lifespan of the 512 S and 512 M, Forghieri responded, 'It was totally positive, especially when we were able to beat the 917s at Zeltweg in Austria, and at the end of the season in South Africa.' In addition the 519 S won at Sebring in 1970, and both the 512 S and 512 M notched up numerous pole positions.

Running a Ferrari 512 S today

In the late 1970s and early 1980s Bob Houghton worked on a number of 512s, but he recalls that many of them – even by that stage – had shed some of their original features. While some of the early 512 Ss left the factory with downstream fuel injectors, the later ones had upstream injectors. Almost certainly those that were converted to M-spec were fitted with the later injectors, which ensured a better atomisation of the fuel/air mixture, which in turn meant more power.

It's hard to know which cars left the factory with the downstream injectors without referring to the original factory build sheets for them. This situation is further complicated by the fact that even in period, some engineering companies offered modified intake manifolds as an aftermarket item, which enabled upstream injectors to be fitted. Bob Houghton said, 'The manifolds had to be changed with the slide throttles, so from an expense point of view it would have been a major issue.'

The valve timing on the later cars was also modified, as Houghton explained: 'The timing was changed only very slightly – it was just the overlap that was changed. But again, that was a performance issue. They obviously found that they got more power that way by playing around with it.'

As has been mentioned elsewhere in this book, the gear shift has come in for criticism from drivers and engineers alike. Apart from citing the problems of synchronising the gear-shift gate with the gearbox gate, Houghton outlined another problem: 'Because the chassis twisted, it was

essential to change gears on the straight! We ran 512s often enough and so we knew exactly how to set them up when they were cold because the engine and gearbox expanded towards the rear of the car, and of course the whole gear shift also moved. When the engine temperature went from cold to hot, the distance from the gear lever turret to the back of the gearbox increased by as much as 7mm, so you had to build this in when setting it up cold.'

Yet another problem was that the engine would throw a rod through the side of the block. 'Because a lot of the engines put rods through the side, most of them got a patch on the block. Well, actually it was a fault with the gear linkage mainly because, with the chassis twisting, drivers would over-rev it. That was a big issue at the time – I mean, racing drivers liked to push them, didn't they?' Houghton reasoned.

As a result of this trend, as well as for logistical reasons, the factory as well as private teams would often swap engines and gearboxes between cars. As they returned from a race and needed overhauling, so one engine might be removed for repair and another installed in its place, so at the next race it might well have a different engine in it. 'On the

BELOW Chassis 1026 is today very much as it was back in period, apart from the M-style airbox and the conversion to a Spider configuration. *(Author)*

question of originality, of course, engines and gearboxes were changed in 512s, and so it wouldn't have been unusual for a 512 not to have the same engine as the one it left the factory with, because it's bound to have been changed along the way. You have to remember that years ago people didn't even think about engine numbers – no one cared. It's only because the values have gone through the roof that people care now, that's all.'

Some years after it had participated in the filming of the *Le Mans* movie, chassis 1026 arrived at Bob Houghton's workshop as a pile of bits. 'We tried to rebuild as much as we could to keep the originality, but it was in a right state. It was in a right state, but we managed to resurrect it, Phoenix-like, from the ashes.'

The chassis is still the original chassis but the engine and gearbox are likely to have been swapped as described above. During the rebuilding process, Houghton ordered new Nikasil liners from Mahle as there was no point in buying new cast iron liners. These were the same as those used in the Porsche 917, although obviously a different dimension, and resulted in a significant weight saving. They did manage to retain the original conrods, and

various other small M-spec upgrades were included in the rebuild. The car is fitted with an M-style airbox, which was done to improve breathing. Although chassis 1026 left the factory as a Barchetta, when the car was rebuilt Mason specified a Spider body. This was done by Church Green Engineering in Dorset.

Looking after Nick Mason's Ferrari 512 S

Ben de Chair has been looking after Nick Mason's Ferraris at Ten Tenths for the last five years, including getting his 512 S ready for a recent demonstration run in the 74th Members' Meeting at Goodwood. 'We won't spend much time on the suspension set-up, because this is just a demo run,' he said. 'But engine-wise, well, we "nut and bolt it" and check it all over, check that nothing's broken on it since the last time it ran.' This is most certainly no casual look over the car; it's more a case of every nut and bolt being checked for tightness or correct torque setting. 'We check that the throttle sliders operate fully,' he added, 'because the little balls and pins in there can sometimes jam up with damp.'

Although Nick Mason and Mark Hales have used this car extensively, it has seen less

BELOW Chassis 1026 waits its turn for a run up the hill at the 2015 Carfest South event on Laverstoke Park Farm in Cheshire, the home of 1979 Formula 1 World Champion Jody Scheckter. *(Author)*

ABOVE Marino Franchitti (seated on the sill) prepares for his drive in the Mason 512 S at the 2015 Carfest South. *(Author)*

RIGHT A container of Millers CVL Turbo, as used by many teams today. *(Ten Tenths)*

FAR RIGHT When your racing car doesn't have a handbrake, an 80mm wheel-nut socket can come in useful as a handy wheel stop. *(Author)*

action of late, which necessitates a thorough examination on this occasion. De Chair explained the start-up procedure: 'You take all the plugs out so you don't labour the starter too much, then crank over the engine to get oil pressure up, checking for leaks on all systems. Then, having fuelled it and added some two-stroke oil in the fuel, to lubricate the metering unit at the ratio 100ml per 10 litres, you also add some CVLT, which is a valve lubricant.

'Then you put the plugs back in and refit the plug leads, which can be quite tricky because they've got rain caps on them, so we need to make sure that they click on properly. And then you run up the fuel pressure. It's got a lift pump in the tank which drags the fuel up to the collector pot and then a high-pressure pump feeds the injectors, so you check the fuel pressure, which normally runs between 9 and 10kg/m.

'With the help of an able assistant to squirt brake cleaner down the inlets to give it an initial fuel, you then fire it up and run it up to temperature, weakening off the mixture as you go. This is because you must start it rich and then go one off full lean by the time it has got up to temperature, and while it's running, checking for leaks everywhere including coolant flow through the radiators. But all the while you're just eyeballing everything to check for faults.'

The big V12 takes around five minutes to run up to full operating temperature, during which time the engine revs are held at between 2,500–3,000rpm. This is to warm the engine through thoroughly, and to make sure that all systems are operating as they should be. 'You might give it a few blips on the throttle and then on a final blip, switch it off,' de Chair added. It is necessary to blip the throttle just prior to switching it off in order to clean the plugs off for the next start-up.

Setting the injectors is an art in itself. The Mason Ferrari 512 S is fitted with upstream

ABOVE **The big 5-litre V12 engine has been prepped: it's the calm before the storm.** (Author)

injectors, which, as the name suggests, spray the fuel upwards. 'There's a bit of a knack to bleeding the injectors which involves tapping the end of the injector pin with a screwdriver ever so slightly. This you do once the engine is being cranked over with the plugs out to build fuel pressure. By tapping this needle ever so slightly – and you only want to move it by about 1,000th, just to let the fuel out and not let any air in – this completely fuel-fills the pipes from the injector unit.'

As has been expressed by some of the 512's drivers over the years, the gear change could be a little troublesome. Seasoned race car driver Mark Hales explained that when changing gears in the 512 the chassis would flex, and this resulted in the gate of the gear lever not lining up with a gate of the gearbox. 'Yes, that's very typical of Ferrari,' added Ben de Chair. 'There's a lot of fine adjustment in the shaft to accommodate chassis twist. You've also got length adjustment, with a left- and right-hand thread on the shaft just behind the gear shift. The gear selector gate is very small, compared to the gear-shift gate, so you've got to have a good centre crossover on the gate, and each gear then has to select in the centre of each

gate. So you can get a bit of binding on the gate teeth if you change mid-corner, or as you're exiting a corner, or just on some unexpected undulations on the track surface. It takes a lot of setting up – there's quite a fine art to it.'

The Mason Ferrari uses Motul lubricants for the engine (Motul 300V Chrono 10W-40 Ester synthetic racing car engine oil), gearbox (Motul Gear 300 75W-90 synthetic racing car gearbox oil) and brakes (Motul RBF 600 synthetic racing brake fluid). In competition the 512 can be fuelled in the pits from either side depending on the circuit, as the car is 'double-capped' with a crossover pipe underneath the driver's legs.

'It looks like a big scary thing and it sounds ferocious,' de Chair concluded, 'but it's actually quite an easy car to look after because it's so big. Everything on it is so massive, apart from the chassis at the back, which is quite flimsy.'

Obtaining spare parts

'We got zero help from Ferrari,' revealed Don Cox. 'I recall one incident where we picked up a crack in the windshield and we couldn't even get a windshield out of them. When we first got into endurance racing with the 512 M, we couldn't

BELOW Few in the crowd at Carfest South would be aware of the many hours of preparation, tuning, checking and testing that go towards getting a car like the Ferrari 512 S on to the starting line. *(Author)*

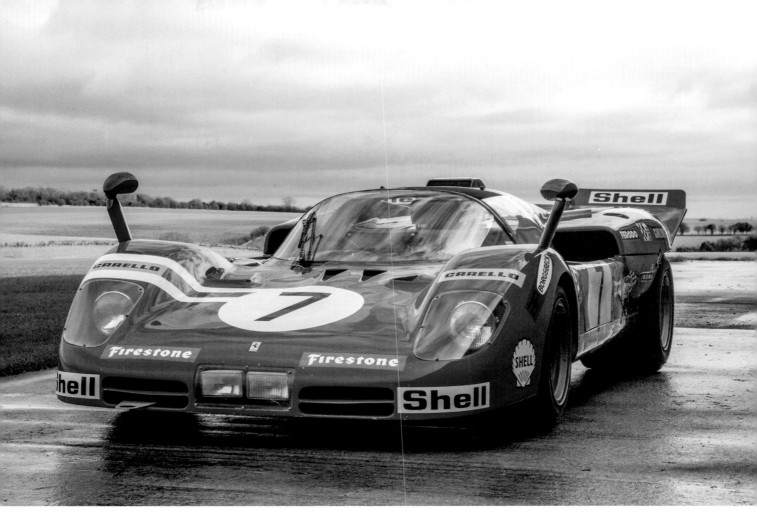

get any help from Ferrari at all, not free help or any other kind. We couldn't even buy some of the spares that we needed. But after we qualified on pole at Daytona and Sebring – ahead of Ferrari, I might add, and, more importantly ahead of Porsche too – we got their attention.'

Cox recalled that they got one engine when they acquired the car (chassis 1040), but to try and run a World Championship season with just one engine is foolhardy, so Roger and Mark travelled to England to try to purchase some more spares. Although the parts they needed wound up being too expensive, they did purchase one more engine and they made a deal to borrow a gearbox because they couldn't afford to buy it. Cox went on: 'We'd also given them a whole list of other parts to get because you can't go to a 24-hour race without a lot of spare parts, but it was like pulling teeth. Although some parts had been bought from Ferrari, they'd never come, so we would telex them every day and they'd say, "Yes, we're working on it." But the parts supply was just very poor. It could be simply that they were

overwhelmed because they had a lot of 512 customers out there, but we had great difficulty in getting parts. There was one occasion when we finally got a half-shaft that we'd ordered, and we were billed for a brand-new half-shaft, but it was a *used* half-shaft!'

Woody Woodard hadn't been around a Ferrari works team at the races before 1971 – the first occasion was at Daytona and Sebring that year. 'I was blown away at how unkempt the mechanics were. I remember them doing pit stops and adding oil at Daytona, with quart oil cans that they opened with a beer opener, and just pouring it in. It was like a pit stop from the 1940s! We had pneumatic wheel nut removers but I don't believe they had pneumatic wheel nuts.'

The blue Penske Ferrari was always immaculately turned out, and, as Woody Woodard commented, 'When we got to the races, the fit and finish on this car was second to none. In fact, that car at Le Mans was the reason we got the Porsche Can-Am project, because Porsche was just so blown away with not only how good the car looked, but how fast it was.'

ABOVE Masculine, muscular, athletic and ready to race...the Nick Mason Ferrari 512 S is rolled out in anticipation of the new season's racing programme. *(Author)*

'We were the first ones to deal in the old competition Ferraris. Although I wasn't entirely alone, I was the first one that honed in on the old Testarossas and the GTOs, but of course back then they were nothing more than used race cars.'

— Kirk White

Chapter Four

The owner's view

When it comes to owning an iconic Ferrari race car, it was Nick Mason who said, 'No one ever bought a bargain.' That much might be true in today's market, but if you'd bought a 512 back in period and you'd held on to it until today, you could argue that you had got a bargain. But in reality such occurrences are rare. That's one of the reasons why the market is so buoyant today.

OPPOSITE 1970 Ferrari 512 M chassis 1034. *(RM Sotheby's)*

Owning a Ferrari 512 today can be enjoyed in one of two ways: either as a driver competing in relevant historic events, or as a collector or investor. Where the owner falls into the latter category, the 512 is realistically more likely to only be brought out on rare occasions, which is a pity, because the Ferrari 512 was born to race.

In period, of course, the 512 was a pure racing machine, and there was no thought of wrapping up such a race car and preserving it for some future time. Racing the car was, of course, the only way in which a pedigree race car could establish a successful record,

and thereby build up a competition record that would in the future elevate it to a level of significant recognition. Ironically, it is the cars that were raced hard back in their day, sometimes to within an inch of their lives in order to win races, that are today identified by the market as being a cut above the rest. The Ferrari 512 S and 512 M, despite the models' relatively meagre record of wins, always attracted attention because of the badge on the front, and because they always competed with the very best in the world.

The answer as to how one can recognise the

RIGHT Brazilian racer and Ferrari collector Carlos Monteverde in 512 S chassis 1016 holds off Martin Stretton in the Abarth-Osella PA1. *(Peter Collins)*

**ABOVE Swiss
Scuderia Filipinetti
512 S chassis 1016
Coda Lunga driven
by Franco Meiners in
the 74th Members'
Meeting at Goodwood,
2016.** *(Peter Still/PSP)*

longstanding qualities in a race car that set it aside from the rest of the pack is complex, and cannot be learned by reading books. Back in 1963, Kirk White paid a visit to Luigi Chinetti's showroom on West 55th Street in Manhattan, and to Ed Jurist of the Vintage Car Store in Nyack, New York. White liked this world of luxurious and powerful European sports cars, and in 1964 he purchased his first Ferrari, as he recalled: 'That place really sucked me right in, and in early 1964 I bought a Ferrari 250 Long Wheelbase California from Jurist and literally used it as my everyday car for the next two or three years. In the spring of 1968 I opened Auto Enterprises, and we did a lot of buying and selling of Ferraris and Porsches, just high-performance European cars. The final step was in May 1969 when I opened my own place down in Philadelphia on 63rd Street, and Roger Penske's agency was just several blocks south of me.

'We were the first ones to deal in the old competition Ferraris. Although I wasn't entirely alone, I was the first one that honed in on the old Testarossas and the GTOs, but of course, back then they were nothing more than used race cars. We found that there was a market for them, and the joy of it was that we were just running the guts out of them and having a good old time. However, the people that are buying them today are just moving them from one sealed vault to another.'

A race car of any era, really, has a competitive life of a year or two at the most, so Ken White and his team were buying them after they'd pretty much done their time. So who was it in those days who was buying them? White explained how he built his business: 'Our operation was somewhat unique in that I put together an informative newsletter on a referral basis and mailed that to just a handful of enthusiasts. We asked those folk if they knew of any other people that might be interested in receiving our newsletter, and asked those people in turn if they could recommend other people. Then we started to advertise the cars, and we grew the list from 84 people in 1968 to over 23,000 by 1973, and we did it all by referrals – no shotgun mailings. It was a terrifically good time.'

The Sunoco 512 S

Kirk White was responsible for sourcing the Ferrari 512 S that Roger Penske turned into the now famous blue Sunoco car driven by Mark Donohue and David Hobbs. He outlined how it all came about:

'Well it was interesting. I'd gone in early one Saturday morning – I guess in June in 1970 – and I remember it was only about 6:30 in the morning. I heard the front door pop open and I thought, oh no, who's bothering me at this hour. It was Roger, and he was on his way to his agency just down the street, and he said, "Why don't you gather up a bunch of your guys, some customers and investors, that sort of thing, and buy a Ferrari 512? We'll prepare it over in Newtown Square and Mark Donohue will drive it. Well, I've got to go. Have a nice day." And he left! That was pretty much the way Roger did things – in a big hurry.

'So I approached a couple of our better customers and asked if they wanted to buy a Ferrari 512, and to go for the World Manufacturers' Championship. The fact that they'd have a chance at the championship with Penske was a very big plus. At that time America had a very disadvantageous tax regime, with the very wealthy having to pay an extortionate amount of tax to the government, so to enter into a legitimate business venture with a Ferrari made some sense. So I wrote a three-paragraph agreement letter to Roger the following week and then it just became a job to find a 512 that wasn't all trashed out, because it was the last year of the Group 5s.

'Chris Cord and Steve Earle had this car, and I knew that Doane Spencer was the chief mechanic. Steve Earle was the guy who started the Monterey historic races, and Chris Cord's grandfather was E.L. Cord, the founder of the Cord Automobile factory here in the United States. So they were terrific young guys who had an interest early on in these Ferrari race cars, and they raced them. Doane Spencer is probably America's most famous hot-rodder. Anyway, Spencer worked for Chris Cord and Steve Earle and their car was running in the Can-Am, but the 512 wasn't particularly competitive, and it looked to be the best example. So we went out to Mid-Ohio when that car came east and visited Chris and Steve and Doane, and we bought the car.' (Jim Adams came eighth in the Mid-Ohio Can-Am on 23 August 1970. He raced this 512 S – chassis 1040 – three times that year: at Watkins Glen, Edmonton and Mid-Ohio.)

'Right after Mid-Ohio, the last race of the season, Doane actually put the car on a trailer and drove it from there straight into our workshop in Philadelphia. Within hours of the car's arrival on the Tuesday, a truck showed up and the car vanished into Penske's shop in Newtown Square, and it came out as the blue Sunoco car that you see today. We'd paid $28,000 for it!'

Mark Donohue, of course, was more than just a contracted driver; he also had a degree in Mechanical Engineering which he received upon graduating from Brown University in Providence, Rhode Island, in 1959. This was an extremely valuable trait for any team owner, as Donohue was able to set up his own race cars and to advise on components that needed improving.

'Don Cox, a former top General Motors engineer, also signed up,' added Kirk White. 'He had quite a racing staff and, of course, quite a racing operation already established going into our deal. I was the registered owner, plus of course the other four in the consortium. The deal was that our company, Kirk F. White Motorcars, owned the car and Penske was responsible for all preparation, getting it to the track, racing it and testing, and our organisation was responsible for all hard parts. So in other words we had to provide all the spares if there was accident damage – and everybody knows we have enough of that,' added White with a chuckle.

The familiar blue livery that adorned the Penske Ferrari was courtesy of his longstanding sponsorship deal with Sunoco, the oil company that started in Pittsburgh, Pennsylvania, way back in 1886. Sunoco had been a loyal sponsor of Penske in his Indianapolis effort as well as Can-Am and the Trans Am. Sun Oil had been with him all the way.

'I can tell you one story that's pretty good,' White recalled with some humour. 'It was early on in the season at Daytona and we'd battled our way to the pole position. I was a rookie in motor sport, and it was just like joining the New York Yankees – I was now with this fantastic team that had snatched the pole from the Gulf Wyer Porsche 917s. I was talking to some people as the qualifying session ended and I walked over to the garage where the car was but the door was down and the windows were painted out and the doors were locked – I couldn't get in! The press was all around outside wanting to talk to Roger and Mark about this great Ferrari that had just qualified on pole, but nobody could get in – I couldn't even get in, and nobody responded to any of my knocks. Finally, after half an hour, the door opened and Dan Luginbuhl came out. He was Penske's press guy, and everybody asked him, "What happened? What's going on in there?" And he just kind of offhandedly said, "Well, they're switching the engine. That was just the practice engine, now they're going to put the race motor in." Of course, no such thing was being done – it was just the beginning of a long string of Roger's psychological ploys.'

Under Penske's management, the Sunoco Ferrari 512 M competed in just five events in 1971: the Daytona 24-Hours, Sebring 12-Hours, Le Mans 24-Hours, Watkins Glen 6-Hours and Watkins Glen Can-Am races. Unfortunately for the Penske team, the Sunoco Ferrari – which was undoubtedly the best prepared and turned out Ferrari 512 in period – only scored a single podium place, that being third at the Daytona race in January 1971.

The Penske Ferrari was sold after the races at Watkins Glen to one of the original investors in the Kirk White consortium, Roberts Harrison. But such was the perceived potential of the Penske Ferrari that, as White recalled, 'Although it was the end of the Group 5 era, we mounted a mighty petition for the FIA to extend the Group 5 activities, and we actually got some ears listening to us. It was just a handful of Ferraris, but all of those wonderful cars were just going to be obsolete. Anyway, we were ultimately unsuccessful in that attempt.'

Woody Woodard added, 'Today the car is owned by Lawrence Stroll, a Canadian businessman and Ferrari collector of note. The car was restored some years back by Bob Houghton in England and it looks good. It's original just as we'd run it, except that Lawrence being such a tall man he had to put a bubble in the roof and a bubble underneath the foot box. Other than that it looks identical, and it's still got my wiring harness in it! It's an iconic car, and it runs pretty well too.'

Nick Mason gives his views on 512 ownership

There's no getting away from it, Nick Mason is one lucky guy. But is owning some of the most desirable race cars on the planet something that can be put down to luck? Perhaps with one car it might be, but to assemble a whole collection I'd suggest not. To add the next car to an already impressive collection one would need to have an understanding of the value of such cars, not in monetary terms, but in terms of the cultural or sporting value of each car and the role it plays in the race car world. Along with this required skill comes the responsibility of

BELOW Nick Mason powers Ferrari 512 S chassis 1026 around the Goodwood circuit during the 74th Members' Meeting, March 2016.
(Simon Hildrew)

preserving, maintaining and presenting these cars for others to see and enjoy, be that in a display or on the racetrack.

So what does it take to find the car of your dreams? Nick Mason outlined how he came across his 512 S: 'As with all my cars, it was a car that I really wanted to drive and, ideally, race. I was conscious, obviously, of the car's history and where they stood in the firmament. When I was first touring in America I met a guy called Bobs Harrison, in Philadelphia, who owned the Donohue car, and that for me was one of the ultimate Ferraris of all time. So when there was the possibility of buying a 512 S, I thought that was a great opportunity. Because it was a big restoration project, and I was actually away a lot at the time, it seemed a sort of perfect arrangement really.'

Ferrari 512 S, chassis 1026, was originally raced by the factory in 1970, but after the Le Mans 24-Hours of that year it was sold to the Belgian Jacques Swaters, who ran the Ecurie Francorchamps racing team. The car was then leased to Solar Productions for the filming of the Steve McQueen movie *Le Mans*, but during filming the car was severely damaged when it caught fire. The unfortunate car was taken back to Paris and stored in the corner of a warehouse and all but forgotten for several years. Towards the end of the 1970s the remains were taken over to Graypaul in

England, who prepared a quote for the then French owner of the car, but upon hearing what it would cost he got cold feet.

So how did Nick Mason get to hear about chassis 1026? 'Ian Webb, a friend of mine, told me about it. The car was looking for a home, and I thought the project suited me because so much work was needed. I paid about £7,000 for it, and that would have been around 1978, because I was actually out of the country touring between 1979 to 1980, and a lot of work went on while I was away. The whole restoration project took two years.'

By embarking on the restoration process, Mason was able to rebuild the car the way he wanted to race it, which, he admitted, in the current climate may not be the accepted course of action to take. So chassis 1026 was converted to a Spider: 'I thought that would be the easiest and most usable racing car for me, which it was at the time. But actually if I do a rebuild on it again I'll probably put it back as it raced at Daytona or Le Mans in 1970.'

At the time of the rebuild, well-known Ferrari specialist Bob Houghton was working at Graypaul. 'Bob then left Graypaul, and I followed him with my car, which I don't think Graypaul were that thrilled about, but I just felt that Bob was my man at that stage. I also went across to Switzerland with Vic Norman to see Herbie Müller, and Herbie sold me a

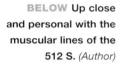

BELOW Up close and personal with the muscular lines of the 512 S. *(Author)*

load of components from his stock of genuine ex-Ferrari parts that I needed to finish the car. With his help we ended up with a car that actually ran quite well.'

Mason tested the car almost immediately after the rebuild was complete. A quick 'jolly' to Dubai for a run in the David Piper series followed in the early 1980s. Did Nick have visions of the 512 having a 917-like reputation that dogged the Porsche in the early days? 'I suppose it's probably slightly more tractable than I expected. I expected a complete monster, although I probably wasn't exactly giving it absolutely everything, but it was remarkably sensible in a way. It did have a tendency to understeer in the slow corners,' Mason admitted.

Although the answer to the question 'Was he pleased that he bought the wreck when he did' was going to be fairly predictable, there was more to it than might have been obvious. 'Oh yes. It's a wonderful piece of history. It looks sort of *Jurassic Park* really, and wonderful for it. I think it's a very important car, it's one of the jewels, and although it isn't totally original a lot of work went into repairing it and making it what it is. It does have history, and even if they were rather blitzed by the 917s, it still represents a very special part of Ferrari history. All the right people were in those sorts of cars.'

Having a race car like the Ferrari 512 S in your garage is one thing, but maintaining it

and running it requires resources. Surprisingly, though, the 512 S has not had a lot spent on it over the years. 'It isn't like one of those small engines that's constantly needing attention. It's a big thing so it tends to run pretty well. Of course, I haven't done thousands of racing miles in it and it was built for long-distance racing, so actually it isn't something that needs a rebuild every three hours.'

In period, when the teams were running in the Manufacturers' World Championship, it was estimated that the 5-litre engine would need a rebuild after every 40 hours of racing. But

ABOVE Back in May 2007 this 1970 Ferrari 512 S (chassis 1006) sold at the 'Ferrari – Leggenda e Passione' RM Sotheby's auction held at the Ferrari factory for a then healthy €2,640,000. Today this vehicle would command substantially more. *(Don Heiny, courtesy of RM Sotheby's)*

then the teams were competing for the World Championship, and they were running it on the ragged edge. 'From that point of view, you could never say the 512 was a practical racing car,' Mason added, 'but they certainly don't need as much fettling as you might think.'

Although Mason felt that his days of racing the 512 in anger himself were probably over, he wouldn't like to see it just sitting in the corner gathering dust for the rest of its existence. 'I've enjoyed it and it wasn't the terrifying car that I first thought. It had such incredible grunt, but it never did bite me,' Mason confessed with a smile.

With the almost unstoppable upward trend in attention created by rare Ferraris, the conversation turned inevitably to values and future market trends. 'Ferrari does seem to be the brand for car collecting,' Mason stated matter-of-factly, 'and the very rare Ferraris with history and a story to them have got to be the most interesting and exciting. But I think, like many people, I'm a bit disapproving of the market when it gets superheated because a lot of people get frightfully excited about cars that they don't know very much about.'

The Porsche 917 and the Ferrari 512 were direct competitors in their day, and interestingly they're competitors again today in terms of value. 'Yes, they are,' confirmed Mason. 'But because the 917s virtually all come with fantastic history, in my view the 512 would be worth a bit less. Having said that, Ferrari has become the *Château Petrus* of cars. Just the brand name seems to make such a difference.'

Values

The period during the latter part of the 1980s and the early 1990s saw the values of classic cars and race cars soar to astronomical levels, only to fall dramatically in the years that followed. In the last decade values have again been climbing steadily, and in the last five years have really climbed steeply. Just recently a 1957 Ferrari 335 S Spider Scaglietti sold at auction for a staggering £24.7million, an auction record. Admittedly only four of these cars were made, but then Ferrari didn't go in for 'mass production' on the scale that it does today, so Ferrari values are always going to be high. In 2013 a Ferrari 250 GTO sold in a private deal fetched in excess of $50 million, but there's no way of telling what it might have reached on the open market.

With this backdrop in mind, are we seeing a repeat of the 1989/90 surge in values, only to be followed by another collapse of the market? Max Girardo, managing director and chief auctioneer at RM Sotheby's, said, 'No, it's completely different. The 1990s market was an investment market; you had lots of loans behind that bubble with people borrowing money to buy cars, and then buying a car but only keeping it for three months before selling it. You don't see that today, because today's market is driven by passionate collectors as opposed to the speculators of the 1990s; in turn, there's a completely different atmosphere, and they're completely different buyers too. The collector car market has reached what I call a "happy place", and it's stabilising, which shows that it's an intelligent market and not a speculative market.'

The market for the Ferrari 512 S and 512 M is obviously very niche, with just 25 cars having been produced, theoretically. In reality the number of genuine cars is a little lower than the 25 units originally required by the FIA, because after they were produced some were dismantled and kept as spares to sell or to repair damaged cars. It's generally accepted that 22 cars were actually completed, with around 16 believed to still exist. Being such a small market means that these cars are extremely sought-after, though they rarely change hands. This doesn't mean that people don't want to buy them. Instead it reflects a type of owner who's more disposed towards holding on to his or her car, rather than a speculator simply looking to 'flip' a purchase for profit.

It would be useful to understand what the profile of the typical Ferrari 512 buyer is, because this would determine whether one sees the car on the racetrack or behind locked doors in a private collection. Someone who buys a 512 because it's a very specialist market would have to know what a 512 is and what it can do, as well as be very knowledgeable about the car's heritage in order to want one. 'An investor would more likely go for more of a bread-and-butter Ferrari,' Girardo added, 'because a 512 is difficult to use properly as it's a more specialised car. So perhaps it would sit well with a racing driver, although it's a handful to race. I can't think of anyone who's bought one as an investment. No one can explain the values of these cars – it's like an exclusive club, but it takes two people to do a transaction, and so it goes on.'

So if these Group 5 Ferraris don't trade very often, how can one calculate a fair market value for them? Comparing the 512 with its contemporaries, such as the Porsche 917, the Alfa Romeo T33/3 or perhaps the older Lola T70, may provide a useful benchmark. Girardo suggested that the Ferrari is on a par with the 917: 'They've always been similar, but they're leagues ahead of the Alfa and the Lola – there's no comparison. Even though the Alfa actually beat the Ferrari on several occasions in period, it's still an Alfa Romeo, and passion dictates strongly in this market.'

BELOW 1970 Ferrari 512 M chassis 1034 didn't find a buyer at the RM Sotheby's Monterey Sports and Classic Car Auction in August 2007. At the time it was estimated to sell for between $800,000 and $900,000.
(RM Sotheby's)

Of course, the best way of gauging market value is to look at the last example sold, and consider that car's pedigree against another 512. In 2005, Ferrari 512 chassis number 1006 sold for around $2 million; the same car sold at auction again two years later for $3.5 million, a 75% jump in just two years. Also in 2007, chassis 1034 was offered for sale through RM Sotheby's with an estimate of between $800,000 and $900,000; however, it fell shy of its reserve and didn't find a buyer. Chassis 1034 was the car driven by Arturo Merzario and Clay Regazzoni that was involved in a multiple-car pile-up at Le Mans in which it was extensively damaged. In May 2008, RM Sotheby's sold 512 M chassis 1024 for €2,090,000 (around $3.2 million), this being the last 512 of any kind to pass through the doors of this respected auction house to date.

There's also some discussion to be had around whether the 512 S or the 512 M is the better car to have, some preferring the earlier S, citing the ugly airbox on top of the M's engine cover. Others prefer the more powerful

and slightly sleeker M, which doesn't have the bulging side air scoops of its predecessor. 'I think there's a difference, but it comes down to the personal preferences of the individual collectors,' Girardo explained. 'In my opinion, a lot of the difference is based on the looks of the car. I suppose that beauty is in the eye of the beholder, but in today's market aesthetics are very important. It's also down to liveries as well, and of course the livery is dependent on who raced it, what it achieved, or whether it raced at Le Mans. So in general, it depends on who you talk to, because everyone has their own view as to which is more desirable. Merzario and Regazzoni drove chassis 1034, a 512 S Berlinetta factory entry, and they were involved in a race-ending accident in the first three hours. It was a multiple-car pile-up which virtually destroyed the car, so all of these things must be taken into account.'

If the 512 is such a rare beast, and it wears the same Ferrari badge on its nose as the 250 GTO, why hasn't it increased by the same stratospheric margins as its older sibling?

After all, less than a decade separates the two cars in age. 'Comparing the 512 with the 250 GTO is an unfair comparison, because you're comparing a GT car with a sports racing car. It's also an unfair comparison because the GTO is in a class of its own. The 512 value has increased a lot more compared to the Alfa 33, and has kept up with the 917. In my view, both the Porsche 917 and the Ferrari 512 are $10 million cars. If you said to me tomorrow, "Go out and buy a 512," I'd say that you need to have $10 million ready,' Girardo commented. That would mean that between 2008, when the last 512 was sold by RM Sotheby's, and 2016, 512 value has increased threefold.

At this level in the market one won't find a Ferrari 512 at a bargain or knockdown price, because both the buyers and the sellers are more knowledgeable today. Consequently, when a 512 comes on to the market it's snapped up pretty quickly. If a buyer hesitates, it may be many more years before another one comes along, with the result that 512s don't stay around for long, waiting for who's willing to pay the full asking price. When asked the $64,000 question, 'Where do you see 512 values going in the future?' Girardo replied, 'I think they're stable. I don't think they're necessarily going to double again.'

BELOW **1970 Ferrari 512 S (chassis 1006).** *(Don Heiny, courtesy of RM Sotheby's)*

ABOVE 1970 Ferrari
512 M (chassis 1034).
(RM Sotheby's)

As already stated, the prices of top-flight Ferraris have risen almost unchecked in recent years, drawing an ever-steeper upward curve. What, though, are the market forces behind this relentless push? Is the 'Ferrari effect' pushing up the prices of other cars in the market? Girardo again: 'No, I don't think so. A handful of cars can't change a multi-billion-dollar industry, that would be very shallow.'

Interestingly, it seems that it's the general anticipation and expectation of society and 'fashion' that's driving this market. 'Fashion' is a word that Girardo used repeatedly in his analysis of this growth, with specific reference to the importance of being seen at events such as the Goodwood Revival, Pebble Beach Concours d'Elegance, Cartier Concours at the Goodwood Festival of Speed and the UK's Concours of Elegance. To this list, one could easily add Salon Privé at the picturesque Blenheim Palace in Oxfordshire, England, and the exclusive Concorso d'Eleganza Villa d'Este, held in the beautiful surroundings of Lake Como. There's also an ever-increasing programme of top-level historic racing car events, such as the Imola, Jarama, Le Mans and Spa Classic races and, of course, the Grand Prix de Monaco Historique. It would follow quite naturally that, if you'd spent a large sum of money on a very rare racing car like the Ferrari 512, you'd likely want it to be seen at an appropriate event. In so doing, you'd also ensure that your car is seen by those who might one day come knocking at your door to ask if you wanted to part with your pride and joy for an even larger sum of money than you paid.

Girardo continued, 'There's more money in the world today. The baby boomers, who dreamed of owning a car like a Testarossa during their youth, are now 50 years of age and have the means to buy one.'

The 'fashion' aspect mentioned earlier refers to the growing interest in the car market in society generally. In recent years, motor manufacturers have launched the new Mini, Fiat 500 and Ferrari 599 GTO, and in so doing they've revived market interest in some much-loved icons from the past. The Ferrari 599 GTO borrows on the heritage of the 250 GTO and the 288 GTO, and this has inspired the market to explore the collectability of these models. This blossoming awareness of cars, combined with an increase in available liquidity, has led to an expansion in the car market overall, which car manufacturers have played a big role in nurturing. 'It's a sort of contagious passion,' as Girardo put it.

Girardo felt that there's a big emotional element attached to such a purchase, despite the high values paid for these cars: 'People buy these cars because they love them, because they look great and because they sound amazing, but it's the end of an era. Never again is there going to be a 5-litre V12 sports racer. There won't be anything of that magnitude again, because if you look at Le Mans today, hybrid cars and diesels are on the rise. And I think that's really something that makes the 512 very special, and that's why I say it's passion that's driving this market.'

In the last big surge in classic car prices during the late 1980s the market was truly global, as the Japanese were strong buyers of high-end classics. The situation today is quite different as the market is where the collectors are, and it seems they're concentrated mostly in the UK, Europe and North America. 'The market today is principally in Europe and America. Today the Japanese are more sellers than buyers, so things have changed,' confirmed Girardo.

FERRARI CHASSIS 1024

On 18 May 2008, RM Sotheby's sold 1971 Ferrari 512 M chassis number 1024, at the 'Ferrari – Leggenda e Passione' auction held at the Ferrari factory in Maranello.

1971 Ferrari 512 M

Lot 317 – Chassis no 1024
Sold for €2,090,000 ($3,234,275) including buyer's premium

Chassis number 1024 was built as a 512 S Berlinetta, but the car remained unsold in 1970 and was therefore not used in its S configuration. Being the 12th car in the total of 25, chassis 1024 was converted to M-spec around late 1970 or early 1971. On 15 April 1971 it was sold to Italian Dr Alfredo Belponer (factory invoice number 1068/71) to be raced by his team, Scuderia Brescia Corse. The team's number one driver, Marsilio Pasotti, also hailed from Brescia and was one of the most popular amateur drivers in Italy, racing under the pseudonym 'Pam'.

On 25 April 1971 'Pam' was partnered with Carlo Facetti in the Monza 1,000km, but the car failed to qualify. A week later 'Pam' was again in action, this time in the Coppa di Shell Interserie race at Imola, where he posted a seventh-place finish in the first heat and a DNF in the second heat due to transmission failure. On 6 June 'Pam' scored a ninth-place finish in the Kent 300 Interserie race at Zolder. At the end of the month he recorded a fine fourth-place finish in the Österreichring 1,000km partnered with Mario Casoni, coming home behind a John Wyer works 917 and a pair of Autodelta Alfa 33s.

July saw further good results for chassis 1024 when 'Pam' finished sixth in both heats of the Interserie 200 Miles of Norisring, for an overall fifth place on the day. An eighth-place finish on 12 September in the Imola 500km was followed the following month with another eighth place in another Interserie race, the Preis von Baden-Württemberg at Hockenheim. At the Paris 1,000km held on the Montlhéry circuit on 17 October, 'Pam' was placed seventh on the grid but an engine failure resulted in a DNF. The 1971 season was rounded off with victory in the Malegno-Borno hill climb.

In 1972, with the rules governing the Group 5 racers having expired, the 512 didn't have too

many events in which it could race, and the car passed through the hands of various owners in the following decades. By this time chassis 1024 had clearly entered the world of historic racing, where it competed in the Spa Ferrari Days, Ferrari Shell Historic Challenge, Coys International Historic Festival at Silverstone, Ferrari Maserati Historic Challenge in America and many others. More recently chassis 1024 has competed in the Le Mans Classic and the Monterey Historic Races, where it enjoyed a good deal of success.

Back in 2001 the car was completely restored in the USA and is today an example of a racer that's remained 'unmolested', and one that wasn't raced into the ground. As the desirability and collectability of these cars has continued to rise, so too has interest in owning them, with the result that many of the 512s that were written off have now 'reappeared', some having been rebuilt from the remains or parts of cars destroyed whilst racing. Chassis 1024 has an 'impeccable provenance', as RM Sotheby's described the car, and remains one of the few 512s that has escaped all controversy. Of the 16 believed to survive, just four 512s remain in original S configuration, the other 12 having been converted to M-spec.

ABOVE On some 512s a slender, discreet vertical fin was added to the leading edge of the front fender, as on 1971 Ferrari 512 M chassis 1024.
(Don Heiny, courtesy of RM Sotheby's)

BELOW This is the view that Ferrari hoped most competitors would see of the 512! This is 1971 Ferrari 512 M chassis 1024.
(Don Heiny, courtesy of RM Sotheby's)

'The 512 M was a car that was satisfying in every aspect and very well balanced. The brakes were as good as the engine, and the engine was as good as the aerodynamics and everything was well balanced...'

— Sam Posey

Chapter Five

The driver's view

It's quite clear from the opinions of the drivers in period, and those who've driven one in recent times, that the 512 S wasn't easy to drive, whereas the 512 M was a much more refined machine. This isn't uncommon when introducing a new race car, because its first season of racing usually reveals areas that need developing – such is the nature of and the time constraints that face the sport. This was no more obvious than in the Porsche 917 in 1969, and so it was with the 512 too, because the 512 M was just that much better than the S-model.

OPPOSITE A trio of 512s resting after a day's racing at the Goodwood 74th Members' Meeting: from left to right – chassis 1030 delivered to Ecurie Francorchamps; chassis 1002 delivered to Escuderia Montjuich; and chassis 1038, a factory racer that was written off in period, this being a re-creation today owned by Paul Knapfield. *(Simon Hildrew)*

ABOVE Pictured on a
run up the hill at the
Goodwood Festival of
Speed in 2008 is 512 M
chassis 1048. This was
originally a factory test
car but was sold to
Scuderia Filipinetti in
1970. *(Author)*

'Through the Ferrari *Gestione Sportiva* [GES, or racing department], the factory had its own team of contracted drivers such Jacky Ickx, Clay Regazzoni, Ignazio Giunti and others,' Mauro Forghieri explained. Of course, over the course of the 1970 season, when the 512 raced under factory colours, Ferrari employed many other top drivers too, such as Mario Andretti, Arturo Merzario, Peter Schetty, Derek Bell, Nino Vaccarella, Chris Amon, Jackie Oliver, John Surtees and Ronnie Peterson. 'This department used, for example, the factory cars chassis 1010, 1012, 1034, 1038 and others,' Forghieri added.

Apart from the factory team, there were a number of highly respected privateer teams, some of which were the Ecurie Francorchamps team (Jacques Swaters), Luigi Chinetti's NART, Ecurie Montjuich, Roger Penske Racing, Georges Filipinetti, Corrado Manfredini, Picchio Rosso, José Juncadella and others.

Sam Posey (NART)

Sam Posey had gone down to Daytona in 1969 to drive a Lola T70 for the Penske team, but he lost his seat to Chuck Parsons at the last moment, as Penske had attracted a sponsor for Parsons. Walking around the paddock feeling let down and rather dejected, Posey spotted one of the NART cars just sitting there, and he went up to Dick Fritz, who was the team manager, and enquired who was driving the car. As it happened, the car was a Ferrari 275 GTB/C, and the driver was none other than Ricardo Rodríguez.

Posey recalled the incident with some humour: 'So Dick Fritz said, "You seem like a likely candidate to drive the 275GTB. Why don't you drive it around the garage, and I'll call Mr Chinetti." So I got in and shuffled it around in the garage, and he said, "You did that very well. You've got the ride." And I was still driving for Chinetti ten years later!' It was the first time behind the wheel of a Ferrari for Posey, and as it happens the Posey/Rodríguez duo finished the race in 23rd place overall, winning the Grand Touring 5000 class in the process. Posey's next Ferrari drive was in a 312 P at Daytona in 1970, this time with Mike Parkes, where they finished in fourth place.

The next race, the 1970 Sebring 12-Hours on 21 March, gave Posey his first taste of the 512 S (chassis 1006), but this race is probably one that he'd like to forget, because unfortunately it resulted in a DNF. It's fair to say that during 1970 and 1971 the 512 was an underachiever, and, having driven both the 512 S and 512 M, Posey agreed with others who felt that it suffered from underdevelopment by the factory. 'It was put together very quickly,' he commented. 'When I started driving the M, I had a long talk with Forghieri and he admitted that they hadn't

really done much work on the S, because the M was a sensational car by comparison.'

The question has often been asked regarding whether the 512 S had the ability to beat the 917, given the Porsche's higher top speed and superior aerodynamics. Some drivers, like Sam Posey, felt that the Ferrari could beat the Porsche. 'It was better at certain circuits, but it wasn't ideal at Le Mans because it didn't have the right top speed. We had the long tail there, but that still wasn't enough. I got to 248mph in practice on one lap at Le Mans when we flattened the spoiler and took it up to a higher rpm through the gears. 248mph sounds really spectacular, but the Porsches were doing 253mph, and that amounts to quite a lot over a long race.'

Although the whole aim of racing is to win, the 512 S did have a reasonably good start to the 1970 season, with a win at Sebring and a second and third-place finish at Monza, followed by a third in the Targa Florio, a second at Spa and another third at the Nürburgring. But as always, in motor sport it's the winner who gets noticed, not the runners-up, but as Posey said, 'It plainly could win.'

The NART-entered 512 S driven by Sam Posey and Ronnie Bucknum (chassis 1014) at the 1970 Le Mans 24-Hours finished in fourth place. Posey recalled the race: 'Vic Elford passed me in the Porsche in a full opposite lock slide, and I thought, "I could never drive

like that." The main reason that Vic Elford went by me on the straight was because he was just going so fast all the way around the track. It really was a masterful performance by him. An hour later, though, he was sitting in a sand bank, so I felt a little bit better after that.'

In a reflective frame of mind, Posey admitted that he had been 'spoilt' when racing for Chinetti, because Luigi had signed some really good drivers. Some time earlier, the author had asked Dick Fritz, the Chinetti team manager, if he could name his best driver in a 512. After a short silence, Fritz said firmly, 'Sam Posey!' Posey's response on hearing that was, 'Isn't that nice to hear? To this day I've just really valued my experiences with the Chinetti organisation – they were so nice to me. We did well, you know. I just wish I could have won a big one for them, but it just wasn't there.'

When the 512 S started the 1970 season, the Porsche had benefitted from a full year of development through 1969, and all its earlier aerodynamic problems had been ironed out. In the same way, when the 512 M was introduced for the 1971 season it had likewise benefitted from a year of racing. Sam Posey summed it up this way: 'If we'd gone up against the Porsches with the 512 M in 1970, we'd have won.'

What, then, from the driver's perspective, was the difference between the S and the M? 'Well, I'm hard pressed to say something good about the S,' Posey laughed. 'The difference

ABOVE This NART-entered 512 S (chassis 1006) posted a DNF in its debut outing in the 1970 Sebring 12-Hours in the hands of Sam Posey/Ronnie Bucknum. Here, racing instructor Roberto Giordanelli gives 1006 a workout in the early 2000s. *(Peter Collins)*

was like night and day. The steering in the S was very heavy, it was like a truck, and the car was difficult to slide or to do anything fast with, because the steering was so heavy. The mechanical aspects of the two models were so similar, and yet a subtle change that Forghieri made to the kingpin inclination made the M so much smoother on entry and so much more stable. The cockpit, too, was all jammed up, which is funny because it looks bigger than the M. It was so tight that my right foot would go numb after about 20 minutes, and I'd have to shift without feeling anything. I looked on the S as a rugged car that was very good. But these were Ferraris, and I loved Ferraris.

'The 512 M was a car that was satisfying in every aspect and very well balanced. The brakes were as good as the engine, and the engine was as good as the aerodynamics and everything was well balanced, there was no extreme. The S wasn't that way at all; it had considerable acceleration, but then the braking was awkward because of the pedal placement. The S was just a car that you wanted to do

your job in and get out quickly, but with the M you wanted to stay in the car indefinitely. When you feel it, and when you've had a car like that, you want them all to be that way. The M just had that quality which is very rare in a car.'

So it was a sad thing that Ferrari pulled the plug on any further development, just when the latest version showed signs of promise. Posey agreed. 'Exactly right, but the other thing was that Porsche had the advantage of doing the Manufacturers' World Championship only, whereas Ferrari was still in Formula 1, and wasn't sure where to allocate its resources – Le Mans, Sebring or Formula 1.'

One of Posey's most memorable moments in the 512 M was his third-place finish in the 1971 Le Mans 24-Hour race. Always willing to acknowledge the role others played, he had this to say: 'It isn't just the car, because the car is part of a system that includes mechanics, tyre specialists and all that. If you don't have all that going on, you're not going to win only because of the car. It depends on all the parts working together. The car is just one part of the whole

BELOW The #12 NART Ferrari 512 M of Posey/Adamowicz (chassis 1020) on its way to a podium finish in the 1971 Le Mans 24-Hours. *(LAT)*

success story.' The Watkins Glen 6-Hour in 1971 was Sam Posey's final race behind the wheel of a 512.

When asked who he liked racing against, Posey again didn't hesitate. 'Mark Donohue. He knew so much about cars, he was such a hard worker and nothing ever escaped his attention. He was just a heck of a human being, and I just felt sick when I heard the news of his death, and I still do; I think of all the things I've enjoyed over the last 30 years, and about my life, and that it's been great living it – and they missed all that. It's silly and romantic, but I just feel bad about it. And these are guys you want to race against, you know – you want to beat Peter Revson, and then enjoy laughing about it later, and not being able to do that is very sad.'

Dan Luginbuhl, Penske communications chief (which covered the function of PR manager as well), commented on Donohue's qualities. 'Along with being the driver and chief engineer on all Penske Racing programmes, Mark was the general manager and all-around helper to everyone on the team. This ensured great respect from all.'

Mario Andretti from behind the wheel of a 512 S

The author asked Mario Andretti for some of his memories from behind the wheel of a Ferrari 512 S. For instance, what got him into racing in the beginning?

'That's a very good question, and I don't know, really, why it captured my imagination at a very young age, because there was nothing within the family that would take me in that direction. It was just something with which my twin brother Aldo and I became enamoured by watching newsreels and reading about it. For the first 15 years of my life I lived in Italy, and of course Ferrari and Maserati were very prominent in the sport, and I just gravitated towards racing. So it was personal drive – I wanted to do nothing else and, as I've always said, I never had a plan B!'

As a driver, he had something special that even some of his contemporary pro drivers didn't have. Did he have any idea what that was? 'A burning desire, I suppose – pride of accomplishment and all the things that drive

you. I had no problem being motivated. Once you taste victory you can't settle for anything else, quite honestly. Sometimes I pushed the envelope a bit much, but I can assure you that you won't win races without taking risks. I was just so hungry and I had nothing on my mind except the will to win, and on many occasions that really worked for me, because I always tried to give 110% whenever I was in the cockpit. That's how I derived my satisfaction.'

His first taste of a 512 came as a result of a call from Mauro Forghieri in December 1969. 'He asked me to come down to Daytona for a test. Arturo Merzario was driving the car there but he had some issues on the banking, so I finished up the testing there. I did a tyre test at Sebring as well, and that helped me to become quite familiar with the car. At Daytona I remember clearly that I put the car on pole – it was in the wet, and there was a big fight between myself and the Porsche 917. I really took a bit of a risk, driving very high on the banking where it was a little bit drier, but when I put it on pole the Porsche stopped trying. But 1970 was the only year I drove the 512.'

Urged to talk about the last hour of the 1970 Sebring 12-Hours, he recalled that 'at Sebring, our 512 S Spider dropped out with gearbox failure with about two hours to go, and as I had my aeroplane there I was going to leave, because I was racing the next day in a sprint car in Pennsylvania. But Forghieri said, "No, hold on, you'd better wait. I want you in the other [Coupé] car for the last stint." I was not so sure about that, because at the time Siffert/Rodríguez were in the lead with the Porsche. But all of a sudden they stopped with a suspension problem. This meant the Porsche 908 of Peter Revson and Steve McQueen was in the lead, but they were only saying over the loudspeakers that Steve McQueen was in the lead, though it was Peter Revson who'd been in the car for the better part of eight hours. Steve was obviously much slower, because he had his ankle in plaster. But the part that actually fired me up was the fact that poor Revvie was out there driving his heart out, and Steve McQueen was getting all the credit.

'At that point I said, "Yes, if it's OK with Giunti," because Vaccarella was in the car and Giunti was ready to go. So I asked Ignazio if he minded if I drove, and he said, "No, it's OK, you go." So that was it. I got in the car and I just went flat out. I think I was something like six seconds a lap quicker than the Revson/McQueen Porsche. The Ferrari actually felt good – quite honestly the Coupé felt better than the Spider, and I think that was the first time that I went through turn one flat out. I was just flying! The problem was, though, I didn't sit very well, because Giunti and Vaccarella were bigger than I am, but I was just determined to go. The worst part about it was that I still had to stop for a quick litre or two of fuel to finish the stint, and at that point the Porsche went into the lead again, and so I had to chase him down for a couple of laps. But I passed him and won the race. It was obviously an amazingly satisfying situation for all of us. I remember clearly that the car felt good, and that's why I was able to just really go for it.'

Driving a 24-hour race meant that you were effectively driving for 12 hours during that time, at the limit. Didn't he find that, mentally and physically, it was too much for a driver?

'In those days we only had two drivers, so in 24 hours we didn't have three or four drivers like they do today, which is a bit like going on holiday. I found, with just the two of us, that it was tremendously satisfying. Physically we were definitely at the limit, and we didn't have all these therapists and support staff that they have on the sidelines now. I remember some of the races where it would take you until the Wednesday after the race to return to normal!'

And what would he say was the most endearing aspect of the car? 'To me, it was a very well-balanced car, and Ferrari was notorious for that because they would do extensive testing. You could be so precise with that car, just repeating lap after lap, which is obviously what you want in long-distance racing. It was really a nice car to drive, for a relatively large car; it was a big displacement car, it had good power and a good gearbox, so the 512 had all of those qualities.'

But did he think that, as a result of being bigger and having a bigger engine, it was more physical to drive? 'No. It wasn't more physical in any way. To me it was relatively easy to drive because of its balance, and that enabled me to settle into a good rhythm. When I fell into such a rhythm I felt that I wasn't taking so much out of the car, and this meant I could drive more smoothly and, as a result, more quickly. To me that was the quality of the 512, and I just loved driving it.'

Derek Bell from behind the wheel of a 512 S

Works driver Derek Bell explained that 'I'd never driven a sports car in my life until I drove in the 1,000km at Spa in 1970, and it was thanks to Jacques Swaters, because I'd met him when I was at Ferrari. I'd driven Formula 3 and Formula 2 as well as Formula 1, but I hadn't got any sports car experience.'

Bell had his first taste of racing in 1964, and within four years had been noticed by none other than Enzo Ferrari, for whom he competed in 1968 and 1969. In May 1970 he was behind the wheel of the Jacques Swaters 512 S (chassis 1030) at Spa, where he was partnered with Hughes de Fierlant. The Ferrari qualified in seventh place on the grid and finished in eighth place.

Bell recalled: 'The Ferrari 512 S was wonderful when I drove it and I was quick, but the only thing I will say, in a polite way, is that the 512 S was a bit truck-like. It had very little feel when you turned. It really lacked feel, and it felt heavy, so when you turned you'd go "One… two," and then it would turn – it had a delayed action. It didn't respond immediately to every touch you gave it, but I think that had to do with the springing. To be honest, I don't think they'd done that much testing with it, because in mid-1969 I was at Ferrari, and I didn't even know they were building it. I knew Enzo and Forghieri more than anybody, and perhaps some of the mechanics and engineers, but nobody let on that there was a 512 on the way.'

At Spa the young Bell had shown great promise, and so Jacques Swaters called him up and suggested that he should do Le Mans that year. Having just done Spa the month before, Bell thought that Swaters would want him to drive for the Belgian team, but Derek was surprised when he learned that Enzo insisted that he would have to drive for the factory. To clarify matters, Jacques Swaters met Bell at Brussels airport after Spa, as he recalled: 'So I said to Jacques that I wouldn't do it, because

I'd left Ferrari, and as Swaters had given me my break in sports cars, I wanted to drive for him. But Jacques said to me, "You've got to drive for the factory, because if you don't I won't get any spare parts, because that's the way it operates." So that was it. I drove for the factory at Le Mans.'

Derek Bell and Ronnie Peterson were allocated the works Ferrari 512 S chassis 1026 for the 1970 Le Mans 24-Hours, but the first time Bell sat in that car was at Le Mans. He and Peterson qualified in seventh place, the second of the four works Ferraris.

'I started the race, and remember that neither I nor Ronnie had ever done Le Mans before. What was really weird was the fact that we weren't given any driving instructions. I always thought there would be a big plan – in the first hour we'll run at such a pace, and so

on. But they just said, "You know what to do." I really thought that, being sports car racing at the Le Mans 24 hours with the Ferrari factory team, there would be a very definite strategy: this is how we start the race and we'll run it like this until we get into a rhythm. Or perhaps you're going to go fast or you're going to go slow, or we'll run you as a hare… But there was no strategy at all. They just said, "You must drive." I guess they were just trying us both out,' Derek mused, 'because Ronnie and I were both unknown quantities in that respect.'

Derek Bell and the *Le Mans* movie

Actual real-time footage from the 1970 Le Mans 24-Hour race for use in the movie *Le Mans* was shot from two cameras, one mounted on the front and one on the rear of a Porsche 908/2.

ABOVE Despite carrying two heavy cameras for 24 hours, the #29 Porsche 908/2 driven by Herbert Linge/Jonathan Williams finished in eighth place, but was officially unclassified. *(LAT)*

BELOW The Ford GT40 camera car being rigged up and tested prior to filming. *(LAT)*

The car was driven by Herbert Linge/Jonathan Williams, and although the car was entered by Steve McQueen he was prevented from driving in the race by his insurers. However, despite being weighed down by two heavy cameras, and being delayed in the pits while having its film canisters replenished each time it came in, the #29 Porsche finished in a credible eighth place. The car was unclassified though, because its sole purpose had been to record footage of the race, and it had therefore not been allowed to participate officially.

Additional action footage for the movie was shot shortly after the Le Mans race had finished, and Steve McQueen was very much involved in this phase. Professional racing drivers lined up for this sequence read like a *Who's Who* of the racing world, and included: Richard Attwood, Jürgen Barth, Derek Bell, Hughes de Fierlant, Vic Elford, Masten Gregory, Jacky Ickx, Gérard Larrousse, Herbert Linge, Steve McQueen, Brian Redman, Jo Siffert, and many more. In total, 44 racing drivers were used in the filming, too many to mention here.

It was during one of the filming sequences that the Ferrari 512 driven by Derek Bell caught fire, causing great consternation in the camp. Derek picked up the story: 'Race cars of that era were known for leaky fuel tanks and there was always a strong smell of fuel in the cockpit. The cars would be taken back to a big workshop across the railway tracks about a mile and a half from the circuit, where they were serviced each night after filming. The mechanics assigned to the cars weren't first-line mechanics because all the good ones were working on the racing teams. They were basically support mechanics. In my opinion, as the filming progressed so the preparation of the cars deteriorated, because I drove one of the cars to the circuit one day. When they started the filming the cars were in top condition after Le Mans, but some of them probably hadn't been serviced since then.

'We had lights on the floor in the passenger cockpit area, but we aren't talking about some modern technology here, we're talking about a huge light about 10 to 12 inches across. This was because they were filming from the Ford GT camera car to see the sides of our heads, so the lights were needed to illuminate us in the cars. Steve and I were dashing past the Ford GT camera car, which was probably doing 100 miles an hour, so we were doing 140 so that they got good vehicle-to-vehicle action footage.

'One day while filming, we'd come down through the shot fast and as I stopped at the Ford chicane to turn around and drive back, Steve McQueen, who was in the Porsche, said, "Come on, let's race back," because he always wanted to go flat out! But I said, "That's funny, Steve. I've lost the clutch, because I can't feel any clutch pressure." So I told him to carry on and I'd follow along in a few moments, thinking I'd get the pressure back by pumping it a few times. I'd actually stopped the engine but I managed to start it in gear, so I was driving back slowly because I was shifting gear without the clutch, and it's a big chunky gearbox even when you've got the clutch working, let alone without it. I was just coming out of Indianapolis and suddenly, as I accelerated, it just went *Boom!*, and in a few seconds I hit the brakes as best I could.

'I'm positive that there was a fuel leak, because it just went *Boom!* in my face. There must have been some sort of an electrical short with the lights, because there was no other reason why something should explode in my face. But when the thing is on fire you want to get out, and of course it isn't like today when you put the brakes on and stop, stick the handbrake on and leap out – this didn't have a handbrake, so it wouldn't stop until it stopped! I obviously had to open the door, which meant I had to release a catch over my head and pull the strap on the door to get out, and of course I intended to leap out…but then I realised that the car was still rolling, so I had to brake some more, but it was *still* rolling when I eventually got out.

'I didn't realise that I was burnt until I got outside and the air hit my face, because then I felt my skin seize up. It was almost eerie though, because there wasn't a soul around, not even a marshal. Then a bloke appeared out of the woods and I shouted, "Fire truck, fire truck … and an ambulance!" Just then a little blue Renault or Citroën ambulance turned up with Sister Brigitte, who was in the movie, and she thrust a needle in my buttocks and said, "You'll soon be all right, sonny, don't worry." They then told me to lie down on the stretcher

inside the ambulance, and the driver shut the doors, then he jumped in and Sister Brigitte hits on the panel between her and the driver, and shouts, "OK, you can go."

'And of course, being a Frenchman he let the clutch out and I literally shot out the back of the ambulance on the stretcher! I remember throwing my arm back and grabbing a bar as I shot out, and of course the driver hears all the kerfuffle going on in the rear and hits the brakes, and I shot back inside. The stretcher actually went out about three-quarters of the way and I'd grabbed part of the framework as I went out. The trouble was, I was the only one to find it funny! The driver came around and bolted the door again and fastened the stretcher so it wouldn't do that again, and we went off to hospital.

'We got to the hospital around 11:30 in the morning and they put me down. I think somebody slapped some cream on my face. Then they all left, and went off to lunch, and they only came back an hour and a half later

OPPOSITE **Not only was this an expensive parking lot, but lined up here were some of the world's fastest racing cars.** *(LAT)*

and carried on checking me out! And then Steve turned up to see if I was all right and that was it. I went home that night.'

Driving a Ferrari 512 today

Brian Redman

Brian Redman never drove a Ferrari 512 in period because he was driving a 917 for Porsche at the time, against the Ferraris. 'I've driven a 512, though. I drove one at Laguna Seca when I qualified it for Derek Bell,' he laughed. 'That was about five years ago. But there's no question that if Ferrari had put half the effort into the 512 that Porsche put into the 917, it would have been a race-ready car.'

Redman went on to echo what others had said about the 512's heavy steering. But all of these things could have been improved through development, he added. The problem was, as Redman saw it, that for Ferrari 'the 512 was their second priority. It wasn't their main focus. That was Formula 1.'

Mark Hales

Professional driver Mark Hales has spent many hours behind the wheel of the Nick Mason

LEFT **Brian Redman in relaxed mood discussing his Ferrari 512 memories with the author at the 2015 Goodwood Festival of Speed.** *(Author)*

512 S. The Ferrari 512 inherited a bit of a fearsome reputation partly due the difficulty that Porsche drivers experienced with the 917. This reputation was unjustly earned, as Mark Hales explained: 'Actually, I didn't find it hugely frightening, I think the point is that the reputation was established as much by the speeds that they did on the tracks that they raced on in period. In reality, it's just a fairly simple mid-engined sports car with about 550bhp, which these days is nothing. The aerodynamics in 1970 were fairly rudimentary and the trouble that you could get yourself into had more to do with the track you were racing on, and the fact that racing at 200mph was uncharted territory.'

During the Le Mans Legends race some years back, Mark Hales was behind the wheel

BELOW **It could almost have been taken in 1971: Ferrari 512 S chassis 1026 leads a trio of Group 5 racers around Goodwood during the 74th Members' Meeting high-speed demonstration run. Sandwiched in the middle is a Lola T70, with a 512 M (chassis 1038) in the background.** *(Simon Hildrew)*

of the Nick Mason 512 S when he had an interesting duel with a 1971 Ligier JS3 DFV. Powered by a 3-litre V8, the Ligier developed around 420bhp against the 5-litre V12's 550bhp, but of course, there was a significant weight difference, which balanced out the performance of the two cars. 'I'd managed to stick the Ferrari on pole position, but I had an entertaining scrap with Willie Green's Ligier. Down the straights, where the 512 should have been much faster because the 5-litre engine had more power than the DFV, it was the Ligier that held the advantage. Admittedly the car that I was driving didn't have the long-tailed body, but it was an aerodynamic brick wall.'

The rivalry between the Ferrari 512 and the Porsche 917 was the stuff of legend. Although the two cars produced more or less the same level of output, it was the Ferrari that was far more stable in its first year of racing (1970) compared with the Porsche in its first year (1969). Hales again: 'The Porsche's engine was considerably more primitive than the Ferrari's, but it got its fearsome reputation because it was so aerodynamically unstable. It had a tube frame, and as a result was more dangerous, whereas the 512 at least had a monocoque. The Ferrari's V12 engine had a narrow-angle cylinder head, and would withstand an over-rev whereas the Porsche engine wouldn't.'

Having spoken with several drivers who

piloted the 512 in period, opinions varied as to how easy, responsive and predictable the car was to drive. As we've seen, Derek Bell considered its steering 'truck-like'. Another driver said they felt claustrophobic in the cramped cockpit (the author, not being particularly tall, can certainly attest to this). When asked about the 512's foibles, Hales had this to say: 'It had all sorts of peculiarities! It may have had a monocoque, but it was no stiffer than any of the other cars of that period. For instance, the chassis would twist when cornering, and when changing gears you had to align the gate at the base of the gear lever and a gate at the gearbox, and these would have to be in synch before the change could be effected. I soon learned that if you got a crunch that didn't sound quite right then you didn't let the clutch out. When that happened, I'd come in and say, "Look guys, I can get first, second and third gears but I can't get fourth and fifth – can you do something about it?" Also, it's one of the noisiest cars I've ever driven. The noise in the cockpit was just extraordinary, and it wasn't exhaust noise. It was just mechanical and induction noise coming back into the cabin from the engine right behind you.'

For the spectator watching from the stands, the 512 is just a gorgeous 1970s sports car, but what was it actually like behind the wheel? 'It was nice to drive,' said Hales, 'but the brakes were useless. How the good guys managed the brakes I just don't know. If you used the brakes as hard as you'd need to on a modern track with all the hairpins, you'd have nothing at the end of two or three laps. I know they tried water-cooling them at some point. The four megaphones sticking out the back – those four white-painted megaphones all at different angles – look just brilliant, and the way it looks overall is sensational. I love that car. You don't hear the exhausts because they're out the back, but the induction creates an unbelievable howl which goes right through your head. But it was a nice friendly old thing. I still love it.'

In the late 1990s Mark Hales was second on the grid in an historic race at Silverstone, but he failed to finish when the engine seized. 'The oil filter collapsed and it nipped up a big end bearing, but fortunately the engine didn't come apart.' Today that crankshaft has been converted into a lamp stand in Nick Mason's office – a little unconventional perhaps but totally practical, and possibly one of the more expensive lamp stands you'll come across.

In conclusion, one should view the Ferrari 512 as a sports racer in the context of the period in which it was designed and built. As with most racing cars of the time, they were in a constant state of development, and when a manufacturer supported a number of private teams they'd frequently supply components with which to upgrade the cars. 'The thing

you have to be aware of with those older Ferraris,' Mark Hales explained, 'is that they were all different – they had different lengths of bodywork, they had different engines, they had different cams. Although the factory wasn't officially involved, they'd send bits to customers suggesting that they try the new components in their cars. This was fairly standard for Ferrari, and they could be forgiven because Porsche threw a fantastic amount of effort and resources at the 917, and the only realistic opposition was the Ferrari 512.'

ABOVE The well-known Escuderia Montjuich 512 M (chassis 1002) negotiates a tight curve in Lugagnano, Italy. *(Peter Collins)*

LEFT Ferrari 512 S chassis 1006 safely negotiates the tricky Molecomb corner on its way up the hill at the Goodwood Festival of Speed in 2009. *(Author)*

'As the desirability and collectability of these cars has continued to rise, so too has interest in owning them, with the result that many of the 512s that were written off have now "reappeared", some having been rebuilt from the remains or parts of cars destroyed whilst racing.'

Chapter Six

The Ferrari 512 S and 512 M chassis record

In period, the 512 S and 512 M produced a mixed bag of results with just a few highlights, which in Ferrari terms is a huge disappointment. In the car's first year of competition, 1970, several privateer teams raced the 512, but in its second year, 1971, it was an all-privateer assault. This meant that the privateer market could get its hands on a world-class sports racer from day one, and so these cars have been traded freely since the early 1970s. As a result, they are today spread far and wide in private hands.

OPPOSITE Ferrari 512 M chassis 1002 was sold to Escuderia Montjuich in 1970, but since 1974 it remained in the ownership of UK collector Robert Horne for more than three decades. *(Author)*

The FIA required Ferrari to produce 25 512s in order to meet the Group 5 class regulations. However, only 22 were completed, which was substantially more than the three Porsche 917s that greeted the CSI inspectors when they visited the Stuttgart plant in March 1969. As has been mentioned, despite a further 18 cars being in various stages of assembly, and sets of spares existing for the remainder, the CSI flatly refused to approve the cars for homologation, and Porsche had to assemble all 25 completely.

Only 16 512s can be accounted for today, of which just four exist in S trim. Although 15 cars were converted to M-spec in period, only 12 of those still exist. The Spider version of the 512 was only available in the 512 S configuration, and there were five of these that raced in 1970.

During the 1970 season the factory utilised nine 512s for its own racing programme, and of course in 1971 they didn't race in an official works capacity. Private teams who raced the 512 in 1970 included Chinetti's NART outfit and Scuderia Filipinetti, who each raced two cars, while Ecurie Francorchamps, Escuderia Montjuich, Gelo Racing Team, Earl Cord Racing and Picchio Rosso raced just one car each. This accounts for 18 cars that raced during the 1970 season.

BELOW The David Hobbs/José Juncadella Ferrari 512 M (chassis 1002) exits Hawthorns during the 1971 Brands Hatch 1,000km.
(Peter Collins)

Individual chassis numbers

Chassis 1002

Finished in striking yellow with two thin red stripes running down the length of the car, chassis 1002 was sold new to the Escuderia Montjuich racing team in April 1970. This team was founded by four wealthy gentleman drivers who hailed from the Catalan region of Spain: Enrique Coma-Cros, Félix Muñoz, José Juncadella and Juan Fernández. Juncadella and Fernández were both accomplished racing drivers of the period and competed internationally, so chassis 1002 was in good hands.

In June 1970 Juncadella and Fernández were placed 24th on the grid at Le Mans, but after rising to tenth place in the race an accident in the 11th hour (130 laps) caused their retirement. Other events that year included the Jarama 12-Hours and the Paris 1,000km, the car finishing in second place in the latter. The following year chassis 1002 competed in the Buenos Aires 1,000km and the Daytona 24-Hours. Prior to the Brands Hatch 1,000km in April 1971 the car was upgraded to M-spec at the factory, and the result in the British event was a fine fifth finish for Juncadella and David Hobbs.

Rather disappointingly the Monza race

resulted in a DNF, so the next race was the 1971 Le Mans 24-Hours, where Nino Vaccarella joined José Juncadella. Placed sixth on the grid, chassis 1002 was looking in good shape as a rolling start was implemented for the first time at Le Mans. The Ferrari gave an excellent account of itself, rising to fourth place, and it even led the race momentarily before a transmission failure caused its retirement once again.

Chassis 1002 led a busy season competing around Europe throughout 1971, but at the end of the season the Group 5 cars passed into the history books. Just three short years later chassis 1002 was sold to an English collector, Robert Horne, who brought the car back to top condition. Horne retained it for 35 years before selling it in 2009 to Dieter Roschmann.

Chassis 1004

The 1970 Daytona 24-Hour race marked the debut of the 512 S, when chassis 1004 was one of the factory cars entered for Jacky Ickx/ Peter Schetty. After qualifying in fifth place the Ferrari was in amongst the Porsche 917s, but it all came to an early end when Ickx hit the wall with 115 laps on the board. Chassis 1004 was returned to the factory, where the car was repaired and converted to a Spider for Ignazio Giunti/Nino Vaccarella to drive in the Monza

1,000km. From fourth on the grid, chassis 1004 finished in a fine second place. The following month the same pairing powered the big Ferrari to third place overall in the Targa Florio. This marked the end of chassis 1004's racing days, as the car was totally dismantled in June 1970 and used as spares for other customer 512s.

Chassis 1006

Featuring an open roof, chassis 1006 was delivered to Luigi Chinetti's NART outfit in time for the Sebring 12-Hours on 21 March 1970. Sam Posey and Ronnie Bucknum were paired together, qualifying the Spider in sixth place on the grid.

ABOVE Dieter Roschmann pilots chassis 1002 during the Silver Flag hill climb in Vernasca, Piacenza, Italy, June 2011. *(Peter Collins)*

BELOW This 1970 Ferrari 512 S, chassis 1006, is seen regularly on the historic racing circuit. *(Don Heiny, courtesy of RM Sotheby's)*

Unfortunately, the car retired with gearbox failure after five hours. Pedro Rodríguez scored eleventh and seventh places in two Can-Am races that year, which accounted for its activities in 1970. Ronnie Bucknum and Tony Adamowicz finished a fine second in the 1971 Daytona 24-Hours, but in the Le Mans race Masten Gregory and George Eaton were forced to retire with fuel system problems.

The car then passed through a number of owners that included Steve Earle, Chris Cord and Otis Chandler. In 2007 chassis 1006 was sold by RM Sotheby's for €2.6 million in the 'Leggenda e Passione' sale at the Ferrari factory in Maranello.

Chassis 1008

This car, finished in red and sporting a roof bubble, was built as a 512 S Berlinetta and sold to the Scuderia Filipinetti team. On 31 May, Herbert Müller and Mike Parkes brought the car home in fourth place in the Nürburgring 1,000km. Just two weeks later, at the Le Mans 24-Hour race, Jo Bonnier and Reine Wisell were involved in a race-ending accident after just 36 laps.

In 1970 the car was sold to the Herbert Müller Racing Team and in early 1971 it was converted to M-spec. In the hands of Gianpiero Moretti and Teodore Zeccoli the car finished in eighth place overall in the Monza 1,000km on 25 April 1971. On 11 July that same year

Herbie Müller loaned it to his friend Pedro Rodríguez for the 200 Miles Norisring Interserie event. As Rodríguez was exiting a tunnel in the first of the two heats the Ferrari clipped the Armco barrier, and Rodríguez was killed in the ensuing accident. There is great controversy surrounding the accident, as he might have been squeezed by a backmarker, but the fact remains that one of the greatest sports car drivers of all time died that day. The car was a write-off, and Herbie Müller removed the chassis and had it chromed for posterity. The original engine and transmission were removed from the car and a replica 512 M was made by John Hajduk for American Rob Dyson.

Chassis 1010

Entered by Ferrari in the 1970 Sebring 12-Hours for Mario Andretti and Arturo Merzario, this 512 S Spider was classified as not running at finish due to gearbox maladies, with 227 laps completed against 248 laps by the winning 512 S. On 12 April 1970 Jacky Ickx and Jackie Oliver finished eighth overall in the Brands Hatch 1,000km. Ignazio Giunti and Arturo Merzario only completed two laps of the 14-mile Nürburgring circuit on 31 May before fuel feed problems ended their race. In July, Jacky Ickx and Peter Schetty finished fifth overall in the Watkins Glen 6-Hour race, but Ickx failed to finish in the Can-Am race that followed at the same venue.

BELOW Jacky Ickx (chassis 1010) waits in the pit lane during the 1970 Brands Hatch 1,000km. *(Peter Collins)*

In August of that year the car was converted to M-spec (the first car to be converted to M specification). Its first outing was the Österreichring 1,000km, where Ickx was second on the grid. Despite a good showing, it retired with electrical trouble. Its next outing was in South Africa in the Kyalami 9-Hours, where Jacky Ickx and Ignazio Giunti trounced the Porsche 917s. Thereafter the car was converted to 712 spec for Can-Am racing.

Chassis 1010 had several first places in the 1971 Interserie, and has since led a very active life on the historics circuit.

Chassis 1012

The life of chassis 1012 started with great promise, when Chris Amon and Arturo Merzario drove the factory-entered car to fifth place in the Brands Hatch 1,000km on 12 April 1970. The following month Nino Vaccarella and Ignazio Giunti scored an unexpected third place overall in the Targa Florio, but the car failed to make the grid for the start of the Nürburgring 1,000km after Peter Schetty crashed it in practice.

At the beginning of June chassis 1012 was completely disassembled by the factory for spares. Later that month the body and chassis were sold to Jacques Swaters, and, now labelled as chassis 1024, the car was used by Steve McQueen in the filming of his movie *Le Mans*. The body panels were fixed to a Lola T70 chassis and used in the remote-controlled crash scene – fortunately the original 512 chassis remained out of this sequence. Herbie Müller purchased the parts from the newly created 'chassis 1024' and reunited these with the original chassis 1012 to avoid any confusion and later duplication. The car has since enjoyed a fairly active life on the historics circuit.

Chassis 1014

Delivered to NART in time for Dan Gurney and Chuck Parsons to drive in the 1970 Daytona 24-Hour race on 31 January. The car didn't finish on its first outing, retiring with gearbox trouble on lap 464. Chassis 1014 next competed in the Le Mans 24-Hour race on 13/14 June of that year, when Sam Posey and Ronnie Bucknum put in an excellent performance to finish in fourth place overall and third in class. NART mechanic François Sicard

converted this car to M-spec for the Chinetti team (see Chapter 3), but it failed to finish in the hands of Masten Gregory and Gregg Young in the 1971 Daytona.

The car was sold to Gregg Young in 1971, his team Young Racers being funded by Young's mother Irene. An accident in the Sebring race resulted in another DNF, and NART mechanic Sicard, who now worked for Young (he still did work for Chinetti), rebuilt the car as a Spider following a trip to Maranello to purchase spares. A first in the 12-Hours of Ecuador by Gregg Young was a welcome result, but the car was destroyed in the Fuji Grand Prix the following year.

Chassis 1016

Scuderia Filipinetti, one of Ferrari's regular customers, purchased this car in 1970. It was finished with a central white stripe which spread to the full width of the car's nose. Mike Parkes and Herbert Müller finished 13th in the Brands Hatch 1,000km and eighth in the Monza 1,000km. A sixth-place finish in the Targa Florio followed for the Parkes/Müller duo.

Although it qualified in eighth position on the grid at Le Mans, it was involved in a multiple-car pile-up on lap 37. For Le Mans it was fitted with a *Coda Lunga* tail section. This car was also one of those used in the *Le Mans* movie.

Herbert Müller entered the car in 1971 for drivers Cox Kocher and Heinrich Wiesendanger,

BELOW Ferrari 512 S chassis 1016 brought back memories of its heyday when it participated in the 74th Members' Meeting at Goodwood in March 2016. *(Simon Hildrew)*

ABOVE The Ferrari
512 S (chassis 1018)
of Georg Loos and
Jonathan Williams
rounds Druids in the
1970 Brands Hatch
1,000km practice.
(Peter Collins)

but it scored a string of non-finishes. It wasn't
upgraded to M-spec, and was sold to Chris
Cord in the USA later that year. It subsequently
led an extremely active life in the world of
historic racing and has, in fact, been more
successful here than it was in period.

Chassis 1018

This car was sold to Georg Loos, perhaps
better known for his Cologne-based GELO
Racing team, with which he campaigned
Porsche 911s with great success. The Ferrari
chassis 1018 was given a Spider body in
red with a rather garish gold stripe and nose
with gold dive planes, and was driven by
Loos himself together with Helmut Kellerners.
Unfortunately, for the car's first race the correct
tyres didn't arrive, and so it didn't start at the
Brands Hatch 1,000km on 12 April 1970.

A week later at Zolder, Loos and Kellerners
put in a spirited performance when they won the
500km race, but apart from a seventh-place finish
in the Österreichring 1,000km in October the rest
of the 1970 scorecard was filled with DNFs and
accidents. The car was converted to M-spec
in 1971 and there followed a string of midfield
results in the Interserie that year. Le Mans was
another disappointment for the Ferrari, as it was
forced to retire with engine trouble.

The car passed in 1971 to renowned Ferrari
collector Pierre Bardinon, and in the mid-90s it

was acquired by the Stieger Family Collection,
where it is currently held. Far from living the life
of a garage queen, this race car can often be
seen on the historic scene.

Chassis 1020

Chassis 1020 was never used in its original
S-spec, but once converted to M-spec for the
1971 season it saw action in the NART stable.
The account of this car's 1971 race results at
Daytona (DNF), Sebring (DNF), Le Mans (third
place overall) and Watkins Glen (DNF) has already
been covered in Chapter 1. The car was sold by
Chinetti in 2005 to well-known Ferrari collector
Lawrence Auriana, who still owns it today.

Chassis 1022

The many lives of a Ferrari 512 S. Delivered to
Daytona as one of the first 512s to race there
under factory colours in January 1970, chassis
1022 was one of several that weekend that
suffered suspension failure on the banking.
Driving it were Nino Vaccarella and Ignazio
Giunti, who retired on lap 89. It was prepared
for Jacky Ickx for the Le Mans test weekend
the same year, but when it returned to the
factory Ferrari received an urgent request for
a 512 from Corrado Manfredini, whose 512 S
(chassis 1032) had just been destroyed in a
fire. The only car that the factory had available
was chassis 1022, so the original chassis 1032

RIGHT Graham Hill prepares to board the NART 512 M (chassis 1020) for another speed run at Bonneville. Note the full-width rear wing now on the car. *(François Sicard Collection)*

LAND SPEED RECORD ATTEMPT

In 1974 Luigi Chinetti senior wanted to attempt several land speed records at Bonneville, and for this he drafted in a couple of heavyweight names. Driving chassis 1020 for the attempts were his son Luigi 'Coco' Chinetti junior, Paul Newman, Milt Minter and Graham Hill. Although some records were claimed, the car blew its engine and it was left to François Sicard to rebuild it.

RIGHT Graham Hill adjusts his goggles prior to commencing another run. Hill told François Sicard, the NART mechanic, that driving flat-out constantly was tiring on the right foot, as one was driving for long periods at the same speed, unlike in a race where the driver would be constantly braking, changing gears and then accelerating again. As a result Hill would alternate between using his right and left foot on the accelerator with which to apply full pressure, in order to achieve a constant speed. *(François Sicard Collection)*

RIGHT This photograph was taken by Sicard when chassis 1020 returned to the Chinetti workshops in Greenwich after its speed record attempt at Bonneville in 1974. A blown left-rear tyre resulted in cables and tubing being severed, which then wound around the driveshaft and shredded the bodywork. These cables and the tubing were so tightly wound around the driveshaft that the car couldn't be repaired on site, and was returned to the Chinetti workshops where it was repaired by François Sicard. *(François Sicard Collection)*

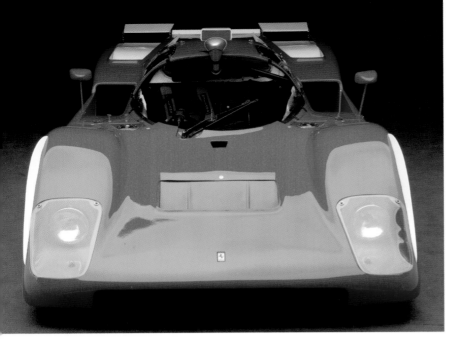

$1.3 million. This car was also once owned by Jean-Pierre van Rossem, the Belgian economist who was jailed for tax fraud in the 1990s. In 2006 the car received its original identity back again and was restamped as chassis 1022, having travelled full circle and endured several bumps along the way.

Chassis 1024

This chassis' career has been covered in detail under 'Values' in Chapter 4.

Chassis 1026

Chassis 1026 was originally a factory racer with Berlinetta bodywork, and was raced as a works car at Daytona in 1970 by Mario Andretti and Arturo Merzario, finishing third. It was driven by Andretti/Giunti/Vaccarella in the Sebring 12-Hours that year, where spectators were treated to one of the finest stints of sports car driving ever seen as Andretti took 1026 to victory. Chris Amon and Arturo Merzario finished fourth in the Monza 1,000km, after which the car was sold to Ecurie Francorchamps, the racing team owned and run by Belgian Jacques Swaters.

In Swaters' care, chassis 1026 scored a fourth place in the Spa 1,000km driven by Ignazio Giunti and Nino Vaccarella, but Derek Bell and Ronnie Peterson retired from the Le Mans 24-Hour race in June 1970. The car was then loaned by Swaters to Solar Productions for the filming of the *Le Mans* movie, where it was badly damaged in a fire. The car was later purchased by Ferrari collector Nick Mason, who still has the car in his collection.

was scrapped and 1022 changed identity and became 1032. Importantly for Manfredini and co-driver Gianpiero Moretti, their next outing was a home race in the Monza 1,000km, where they finished ninth.

Under Corrado Manfredini's stewardship, chassis 1032 was the overall winner in the Trieste-Opicina hill climb. The car then scored a mixed bag of results for the remainder of the 1970 season, including Interserie races, as well as first place in the Golden Race at Fuji for Manfredini and Moretti. The car returned to the factory in December that year to be converted to M-spec, but due to industrial unrest the work could not be completed in time. Instead chassis 1050 was sold to Manfredini, with 1032 going to Scuderia Filipinetti for 1971.

Chassis 1032 passed through numerous owners, and in 1989 was sold by Christie's for

Further details of Chassis 1026's career have been covered in detail in various other chapters of this book.

Chassis 1028

For reasons known only to those involved at the time, when NART took delivery of 1028 they swapped chassis tags between their old 1006 and the new 1028 chassis. The well-raced chassis 1006 was re-tagged as 1028 and sold to David Weir, whereas the newly delivered 1028 was given the old 1006 chassis plate and continued to be raced by NART throughout the 1971 season.

Although the car had been sold to Weir, it was entered in races under a variety of different names. Entered by David Piper for the 1971 Le Mans 24-Hours, chassis 1028 finished in fourth place amidst one of the race's highest attrition rates for years. But credit must be given where credit is due, and David Weir and co-driver Chris Craft drove an impressive, steady race in order to still be there after 24 hours of racing.

Chassis 1030

This car led a very active and somewhat successful racing life in period, in 512 terms. Sold to Ecurie Francorchamps, and wearing its familiar yellow livery, chassis 1030 was driven to eighth place in the Spa 1,000km by Derek Bell and Hughes de Fierlant on 17 May 1970. It went on to finish fifth at that year's Le Mans race (with long tail) and came home in sixth place in the Kyalami 9-Hour at the end of the season.

The 1971 season started where the previous season left off, with a sixth-place finish in the Buenos Aires 1,000km, but the Daytona 24-Hour race ended with a DNF. Although this car scored another DNF at Le Mans, Hughes de Fierlant took it to victory in the Benelux Cup race at Zolder in July 1971, and a sixth place followed at Watkins Glen the same month for Alain de Cadenet and Lothar Motschenbacher. During the course of 1971 the car was converted to M-spec at the factory. In May 1972 Willie Green scored a fine second place overall in the Silverstone Interserie race. Early owners included Nigel Corner, Anthony Bamford, Philip Dowell, Nigel Chiltern-Hunt and several others.

Chassis 1032

As a result of the destruction of chassis 1022, Corrado Manfredini was sold chassis 1032 in its place, the history of which is detailed under chassis 1022 earlier in this chapter.

Chassis 1034

Originally manufactured as a 512 S Berlinetta, this works car was entered in the 1970 Le Mans 24-Hour, where it was driven by Arturo Merzario and Clay Regazzoni. It was totally destroyed in the multiple-car pile-up on lap 38, after which the wreck was sent back to the factory where whatever could be salvaged was removed from the chassis, which was then written off. The engine was later installed in chassis 1010.

This is where it gets interesting, because in the mid-1980s a replica was built using a collection of spares and other genuine Ferrari bits, the engine from 1034 and a new chassis

BELOW Willie Green (J.C. Bamford Excavators) is seen here driving chassis 1030 on his way to winning the first Interserie heat at Silverstone in 1972 in torrential rain. *(Peter Collins)*

from a private builder. The factory, though, does not recognise this car, as 1034 was written off in period and the car as it exists today remains a replica, although it does race and has been seen at the Goodwood Festival of Speed.

Chassis 1036

Created as a 512 S Berlinetta, this car served as test and backup car for the works team. It was sold in June 1970 to Ecurie Francorchamps *sans* engine and used in the shooting of the movie *Le Mans*, after which it was sold on to Herbert Müller Racing. Müller had the car converted to M-spec in 1972. In 1974 the car was again converted, this time for racing in the Can-Am series, and was fitted at various times with 5-litre, 5.7-litre and

7-litre engines, resulting only in midfield finishes at best. In 1978 it was converted back to Berlinetta M-spec and used in historic racing.

Chassis 1038

This 512 S Berlinetta started life as a works car, and first saw action in the 1970 Spa 1,000km on 17 May. Driven by Jacky Ickx and Peter Surtees, it finished second to the Porsche 917 of Siffert/Redman. The next race was to be its last, as the car – driven this time by Jacky Ickx and Peter Schetty – was totally destroyed in an accident at Le Mans on lap 142, when Ickx had a brake lock-up. It was raining heavily at the time, and despite having risen as high as second place it was just one more Ferrari casualty at this event, which was completed by

RIGHT Paul Knapfield gives Ferrari 512 M chassis 1038 a workout. (Peter Collins)

just two of the eleven 512s that had started the race. The factory wrote off this chassis number. In 1990 a replica of this car was built by Bob Houghton, and is today raced by Paul Knapfield in events such as the Silverstone Classic.

Chassis 1040

This 512 S Spider was sold new to Chris Cord and Steve Earle in the USA. Initially driven by Jim Adams, it scored some mediocre results in the Can-Am series that year. After the last Can-Am race in 1970 it was purchased by Kirk White to be raced by the Penske team, its career with whom is recorded at various places throughout this book.

After the 1971 season it was sold to Roberts Harrison (one of the original Kirk White consortium), who sold it to Swiss racer Peter Heuberger, who in turn sold it to Carlos Monteverde. There were financial complications and the car was impounded, until eventually Canadian billionaire and Ferrari collector Lawrence Stroll acquired it for a reported $1.7 million. The car is today campaigned regularly in historic races.

Chassis 1042

This factory 512 S Spider had a reasonably successful career in period, despite scoring a DNF (head gasket) in its debut outing in the 1970 Sebring 12-Hours in the hands of Jacky Ickx and Peter Schetty. Ignazio Giunti, Nino Vaccarella and Chris Amon were more fortunate in the Monza 1,000km in April, when they finished in second place, having started from fourth on the grid. In the Nürburgring 1,000km on 31 May, John Surtees and Nino Vaccarella finished in third place, the same result recorded by Mario Andretti and Ignazio Giunti in the Watkins Glen 6-Hours in mid-July. Andretti also finished in fifth place in the Can-Am race held at the same venue. Arturo Merzario and Ignazio Giunti recorded a DNF in the Imola 500km owing to a broken gear lever.

In 1971 the car was sold to well-known Ferrari collector Anthony Bamford, who kept it until 1995, when he sold it to Giuseppe Lucchini.

Chassis 1044

One of the most actively campaigned 512s in 1970, this factory car scored a seventh overall in the Spa 1,000km with Merzario/Schetty and a DNF at Le Mans with Giunti/Vaccarella, before being converted to M-spec later that year. In 1971 it was sold to Herbie Müller, and finished fourth in the Brands Hatch 1,000km in the hands of Müller/Herzog. The same pairing finished sixth in the Monza 1,000km. The Spa 1,000km was less successful, when Müller/Herzog finished 15th overall. There followed a string of three dismal results, with a DNF at the Nürburgring, an accident at the Österreichring and another DNF at the Norisring Interserie race. Müller retired from the Norisring race out of respect for his friend Pedro Rodríguez, who

BELOW Unfortunately, Cox Kocher failed to start in the 1974 Silverstone Interserie when his Herbert Müller-entered 512 M (chassis 1044) encountered engine problems, which this photo would seem to confirm. *(Peter Collins)*

ABOVE In this image
of the #7 Filipinetti
512 M (chassis 1048)
in the pits at Le Mans
in 1971, one can see
the revised windscreen
shape compared with
other 512s. (LAT)

was killed in this race driving Müller's other
Ferrari 512 (chassis 1008). Further races in
1971 included Watkins Glen, Mid-Ohio, Road
America, Donnybrooke and Hockenheim.

This car was used extensively by Müller in the
1972 Interserie, but at the Nürburgring race in
September it was badly damaged and burned,
but repaired and put back into action. Throughout
1973 Müller used this car in various hill climbs and
the Interserie, this time with many first places. In
fact chassis 1044 was still racing in the Interserie
in 1975. In 1999 it was sold by Gregor Fisken for
$1.4 million to Dutch Ferrari collector John Bosch,
who raced it in historic competitions.

Chassis 1046

Immediately after homologation this car was
disassembled for parts, with the body and
chassis being sold to Herbert Müller Racing.
In October 1971 Müller proceeded to build the
car up with *Coda Lunga* (long tail) bodywork,
using parts recovered from chassis 1008 (the
car in which Pedro Rodríguez died) and some
additional parts purchased from the factory.
It remained unraced, though, and was later
offered to renowned Ferrari collector Pierre
Bardinon. Since the late 1970s this car has
participated in regular historic race meetings.
It was bought by Ferrari collector and historic
racer John Giordano in 1992, who continued to
race it and show it at various concourse events
right up until 2012.

Chassis 1048

Chassis 1048 remained a factory test and
back-up car, and was sold to Scuderia Filipinetti
late in 1970. Now converted to M-spec, Ronnie
Peterson had a big accident in it during practice
for the Buenos Aires 1,000km on 10 January
1971. The crew were able to rebuild the car

and Jo Bonnier/Mike Parkes took seventh place overall in the race. The car did not arrive for the next race, the Daytona 24-Hour race.

Prior to the Le Mans race in 1971, Mike Parkes – who worked for Filipinetti as both engineer and driver – extensively modified chassis 1048, grafting into place a Porsche 917 windscreen. This on its own required much reworking of the cockpit shape and roof. Parkes also fitted a full-width rear wing, and the car became known as the 512 F ('F' for Filipinetti). Unfortunately all of this work came to naught as the car posted a DNF at Le Mans, but Parkes did score a 13th-place finish with it at Riverside in 1972.

Filipinetti sold the car to David Keller, a handbag manufacturer, while Robert 'Bob' Donner is listed as owning the car as far back as 1976. In 1992 Donner sold it to Tom Hollfelder, an electronics equipment manufacturer, who raced it extensively all over North America.

Chassis 1050

Due to industrial strikes, Ferrari could not complete chassis 1032 for Corrado Manfredini, who was sold chassis 1050 instead, which had already been converted to M-spec. When chassis 1032 was eventually completed it was sold to Scuderia Filipinetti (see Chassis 1032 in this chapter). On 25 April 1971 Manfredini and Giancarlo Gagliardi participated in the Monza 1,000km with chassis 1050, but retired with fuel pump problems. There followed a string of three race failures the same year, with a DNS at the Imola Interserie, a DNF at the Spa 1,000km and a DNF at Le Mans. Manfredini scored a 17th-place finish in the Imola 500km in September 1971.

Not much is recorded of this car's activities through the 1980s, and in 1995 it was acquired by noted Ferrari driver and collector Marc Caveng.

Conclusion

As the 1971 season drew to a close, it brought down the curtain on one of the richest periods of motor racing known to date. The Ferrari 512 was a latecomer to the Group 5 party, which was dominated by the Porsche 917s, but despite the Porsche's superiority there was always an expectation that Ferrari could turn the tables at any moment. With the above in mind, and in spite of the fact that Porsche almost always came out on top, you can't talk about the one car without mentioning the other. Ask anyone who worked in the pits at races during this period and they'll tell you that a racing car is never really complete – that there's always more work to be done to make it better, faster, and safer…

LEFT Ecurie Francorchamps Ferrari 512 M chassis 1030 languishing in the paddock at the Goodwood Festival of Speed 2015. (Author)

Index

Abarth-Osella PA1 114
Adamowicz, Tony 33-35, 45-47, 100, 130
Adams, Jim 47, 100, 116
Aerodynamics 12, 49, 55-56, 58, 62, 96, 127, 129, 137
 wings 101, 103-104
Ahrens, Kurt 13-14, 27
Airbox 60-61, 74, 106, 122
Alfa Romeo 41, 47, 94
 Montreal 83
 33/3 18, 32, 38, 40, 47, 121, 123, 125
Alfisti 40
AMC Javelin 100, 103-104
Amon, Chris 21-22, 128
Andretti, Mario 17-19, 21, 30, 32, 37, 100, 119, 129, 131-132
Andretti, Aldo 131
Attwood, Richard 13, 134
Audi 99
Autodelta 125
Auto Enterprises 115

Barth, Jürgen 134
Bell, Derek 26-28, 30-31, 38, 41-42, 45, 128, 132-135, 137-138
Belponer, Dr Alfendo 125, 148
Beltoise, Jean-Pierre 32
Blenheim Palace Salon Privé 124
Body and design 54-63
Bodywork 54-63, 67, 78
 Barchetta 107
 Berlinetta 122, 125
 Coupé 58, 131-132
 engine cover 14, 56, 59-60
 fibreglass 54, 101
 front fender 62, 125
 long-tail (Coda Lunga) 12, 27, 62, 115, 129
 short-tail 12, 30
 Spider 18, 22, 29, 32, 58, 61, 106-107, 118, 132, 142
 tail end 60
Bonneville 147
Bonnier, Joakim 27, 32, 40
Bott, Helmuth 11
Brakes 81-82, 101-102, 127, 138-139
Brands Hatch 1,000km race 1970 20-22, 144, 146; 1971 38-40, 142
Brescia Corse 47
Brigitte, Sister 135
Britt, Bloys 103
BRM Chevrolet P167 47
Bucknum, Ronnie 18-19, 27-28, 33-35, 37-38, 48, 96, 99, 129
Buenos Aires 1,000km race 1971 32
Bussi, Giancarlo 16, 70, 94

Cahier, Bernard 45
Caliri, Giacomo 16, 70, 94
Can-Am series 12, 32, 47-49, 100, 111, 116

Carfest South, Cheshire 2015 107-108, 110
Casoli 54
Casoni, Mario 47, 125
Chaparral 62, 103
Chassis 66-68, 100
 numbering 66
 tubular space frame 12, 66, 100
Chassis records
 1002 142-143
 1004 143
 1006 143-144
 1008 144
 1010 144-145
 1012 145
 1014 145
 1016 145-146
 1018 146
 1020 146
 1022 146, 148
 1024 125 148
 1026 148
 1028 149
 1030 149
 1032 149
 1034 149-150
 1036 150
 1038 150-151
 1040 151
 1042 151
 1044 151-152
 1046 152
 1048 152-153
 1050 153
Chevrolet 48, 62, 103
 Camaro 100
Chevron B6, B8 and B16 19
Chinetti, Luigi 15, 27, 94-96, 99, 115, 128-129, 147
Chinetti Jr, Luigi 'Coco' 96, 147
Church Green Engineering, Dorset 107
Cigala & Bertinetti 54
Cockpit 58, 61, 66, 77, 84-87, 130, 134, 138
 access 85
 controls 87
 dashboard instruments 85-87
 doors 84-85
 foot well 85-86
 forward vision 85
 gear lever 76-77, 106
 interior 84-87
 pedals 74, 82
 rear-view mirrors 58-59, 85, 87
 roof bulge 59
 seating 58, 85
 steering wheel 79, 85-87
 switchgear 87
 ventilation 58, 84, 87
 windscreen 152
 windscreen washer/wiper 87, 91

Concorso d'Eleganza Villa d'Este 124
Concours of Elegance, UK 124
Cooling systems 75-76, 139
 air inlets, intakes and scoops 12, 57, 61-62, 75
 brakes 82
 radiators 56, 63, 66, 71, 74-75
Cord Automobiles 116
Cord, Chris 100, 116
Cord, E.L. 116
Cox, Don 62, 101, 103-104, 110-111, 116
Coys International Historic Festival 125
Craft, Chris 42, 45
Crashes and accidents 17-20, 22, 27-28, 32-34, 36-38, 40, 47, 84, 94, 101, 104, 118, 122, 125, 127, 133-135, 141, 150
CSI 10-13, 142

Daytona 24-Hours race 78, 96, 98, 100, 103; 1970 14-17, 53, 94, 119; 1971 7, 31-37, 49, 99-101, 103-104, 111, 117
de Cadenet, Alain 45-46, 48
de Chair, Ben 107, 109-110
de Fierlant, Hughes 26-27, 29-32, 45-46, 132-134
Delamont, Dean 11-12
di Palma, Rubén Luis 32
Donohue, Mark 32-38, 43-45, 47-48, 58, 100, 102-104, 115-116

Earl, Bob 138
Earl Cord Racing 142
Earle, Steve 100, 116
Eaton, George 47-48
Ecurie Francorchamps 27, 30, 118, 127-128, 133, 142, 153
Edmonton 116
Electrical system 90-91
 battery 87, 90-91
 distributor 70-71, 73
 ignition system 101
 spark plugs 71
 wiring harness 101
Elford, Vic 13, 22, 26-28, 33, 40-41, 45, 129, 134
Engine 106, 109, 127
 head torque settings 72
 lubrication 73-74, 110
 starting 71, 109
Engines
 Chevrolet 104
 Chevrolet Trans-Am 105
 Ferrari V-12 12, 51-52, 68-74
 Ferrari 6.9=litre Can-Am 68
 Ferrari 375 Plus F1 52, 68
 Traco-prepared 32, 34, 44, 102, 104-105
Escuderia Montjuich, 27, 127-128, 139, 141-142
Exhaust system 70, 74

Facetti, Carlo 125
Fantuzzi, Gherardo 55
Farina 66
Fastest qualifying times 22
Fastest race laps 35
Fernandez, Juan 27
Ferrari
　250GT Spider California 67
　250 GTO 67, 113, 115, 120, 122-124
　250 LM 10, 17
　250 LWB California 115
　250 Testarossa 66, 112, 115
　275 GTB 67; 275 GTB/C 17, 95, 128
　275 LM 95
　288 GTO 124
　312P 12-13, 17, 32, 42, 55, 95, 128
　312 PB 31-32, 37-38, 40, 42, 47
　330 P4 55, 66
　335 S Spider Scaglietti 120
　365 GTB/4 Daytona 17, 67, 95
　375 F1 52, 68
　375 Plus 68
　512 M 12 et seq.
　512 S 12 et seq.
　512 S Modulo concept 68
　599 124
　612/612 P Can-Am 53, 55, 66
Ferrari, Enzo 7, 12, 52, 66, 132
Ferrari Gestione Sportive (GES) 128
Ferrari Maserati Historic Challenge 125
Ferrari Shell Historic Challenge 125
FIA 117, 121
　International Sporting Code 12, 55, 68, 84
　Recognition Form 54
　rules and regulations 10-11, 52, 55, 79, 81,
　　84, 89, 125, 142
Fiat 500 124
Filipinetti, Georges 21-22, 27, 128
Fire extinguisher system 91
Florini, Gaetano 94
Ford 11, 14
　GT40 10-11, 134
Forghieri, Mauro 12-16, 19, 32, 49, 52-56,
　62, 66-67, 76, 91, 94, 96, 102, 105, 128,
　131
Formula 1 12, 26, 31, 41, 51-53, 107, 130,
　132, 137
Formula 2 132
Formula 3 132
Franchitti, Marino 108
Fritz, Dick 15-18, 28, 34-35, 43, 45, 92,
　95-96, 100, 128-129
　on NART's race strategy 98-99
Fuel system and tanks 16, 86-89, 101-102,
　110, 134
　air vents 66
　bladders 66, 76, 78, 85, 88
　filler 88-89
　injection system 70, 73, 92, 105-106,
　　109-110
　metering unit 74
　refuelling system 88, 101-102, 110

Gagliardi, Giancarlo 40-42
Garcia-Veiga, Nestor 32
Gelo Racing Team 142
General Motors (GM) 103

Geneva Motor Show 1970 68
Giordanelli, Roberto 99, 129
Girardo, Max 120-124
Giunti, Ignazio 13, 17-19, 22, 25-32, 119,
　128, 131-132
Goodwood 74th Members' Meeting 2016
　52-53, 107, 115, 117, 127, 137, 145
Goodwod Festival of Speed 124; 2008 128;
　2009 139; 2015 137, 153
Goodwood Revival 14; 2007 11
Gosselin, Gustave 32
Grand Prix de Monaco 12
Graypaul 118
Green, Willie 138, 149
Gregory, Masten 18, 35, 37-38, 47, 96,
　100, 134
Group 4 racing 9-10, 12
Group 5 racing 10, 12, 14, 32, 40-42, 47,
　52-54, 87-88, 116-117, 121 125, 137,
　142, 153
Group 6 racing 10, 38, 40, 42
GT Manufacturers' Championship 10
Guerra, Giancarlo 66
Gulf Ford GT40 11
Gulf Wyre Porsche 917 17, 22, 25, 116
Gurney, Dan 15-17, 94, 97, 100

Hales, Mark 107, 110, 137-139
Handling 76, 96
Harrison, Robert 'Bobs' 117-118
Hayden Williams Sportsmanship
　Award 37
Hill, Graham 96, 147
Hendricks airbase circuit 18
Herzog, René 38, 40-42, 47
Hezemans, Toine 18, 38
Historic racing 114, 116, 124-125, 139, 143
Hobbs, David 32-35, 38-40, 43-45, 58, 86,
　100, 102-103, 142
Hockenheim Preis von Baden-Wuertternberg
　125
Holman & Moody 101
Horne, Robert 141
Houghton, Bob 79, 105-107, 117-118

Ickx, Jacky 17-19, 21-22, 26-27, 29-31, 38,
　40, 42, 49, 128, 134, 144
Imola 124
　Coppa di Shell Interserie 1971 125
　500km race 1971 125
Indianapolis 116
International Championship for Manufacturers
　1970 20
Interserie series 49, 125, 149, 151
Iori, Nereo 96-98

Jarama 124
J.C. Bamford Excavators 149
Jones, Parnelli 100
Juncadella, José 27, 32, 35, 38-40, 43, 45,
　47, 128, 142
Juncadella team 32, 38
Jurist, Ed 115

Kauhsen, Willy 41
Kellerners, Helmut 27
Kinnunen, Leo 25

Kirk F. White Motorcars 116
Knapsfield, Paul 114, 127, 150
Kocher, Cox 41-42, 151
Kyalami 9-Hour race 1965 10; 1969 12; 1970
　30, 54

Laguna Seca 137
Laine, Hans 22
Lampredi, Aurelio 52
Lancia 83
Land speed record attempt 147
Lap records 32
Larrousse, Gérard 40, 45 134
Launch 12-13
Le Mans movie 107, 118, 133-135
Le Mans 124
　Classic 125
　Legends race 137
　24-Hours race 11, 16, 53, 55, 77, 94, 96,
　　98, 100, 122, 129; 1932 94; 1934 94;
　　1949 94; 1966 10; 1968 14; 1969 10,
　　13-14; 1970 20, 27-29, 62, 94, 96, 99,
　　104, 118, 129, 133; 1971 42-47, 49, 96,
　　101, 103-104, 111, 117, 130, 152
　rolling start 42
Lesovsky, Lujie 101
Lights 12, 76, 89-90, 134
Ligier, JS3 DFV 138
Linge, Herbert 134
Liveries 122
Lola T70 10, 19, 53, 121, 128, 137
Loos, Georg 21-22, 27, 29, 42, 146
Lugagnano 139
Luginbuhl, Dan 117, 131

Maioli 66
Malegno-Borno hill climb 1971 125
Manfredini, Corrado 16-17, 22, 27, 40-42,
　128
Marelli, Gianni 16, 94
Marko, Helmut 45, 47
Martin, Paolo 68
Martini Porsche 917 41
Maserati 66, 125,131
Mason, Nick 52-53, 92, 105, 107-111, 113,
　117-120, 137-139, 148
Matra 32
McLaren M8F 49
McQueen, Steve 18-19, 118, 131-132, 134-
　135, 137
Mercury Cougar 16
Merzario, Arturo 13, 17-19, 22, 27, 35, 40,
　87, 119, 122, 128, 131
Mid-Ohio 116
Mini 124
Minter, Milt 96, 147
Monterey historic races 116, 125
Monteverde, Carlos 114
Monthléry circuit Paris 1,000km race 1971
　125
Monza 1,000km race 1970 22, 25, 129;
　1971 40-41, 125
Moretti, Gianpiero 16-17, 20, 41
Moss, Stirling 100
Motschenbacher, Lothar 48
Müller, Herbert 21-22, 25, 27, 38, 40-42, 47,
　118, 151

NART (North American Racing team)/Chinetti
 – *throughout*
  the team 94-100
Neubauer, Alfred 103
Newman, Paul 96, 147
New York Times 103
Nicosia, Emanuele 56
Norisring Interserie 200 Miles of Nürnberg
 1971 47, 125
Norman, Vic 118
Nose section 12, 54, 57, 76
Nürburgring 1,000km race *1969* 13; *1970*
 27, 129; *1971* 42

Oil system 71, 73-76, 95, 100
Oliver, Jackie 21-22, 35, 42, 45, 128
Originality 107
Österreichring 12
 1,000km race *1969* 13; *1970* 30;
 1971 47, 125

Pairetti, Carlos 32
Parkes, Mike 21-22, 25, 28, 32, 40, 128
Pasotti, Marsilio 'Pam' 47, 125, 148
Parsons, Chuck 15-16, 37
Pebble Beach Concours d'Elegance 124
Penske, Roger 32, 34, 36, 44-45, 83, 97-98,
 100, 103, 111, 115
Penske Racing Team 32, 43-44, 58, 100-
 105, 125
 fuel rig 101
 workshop 104
Penske Sunoco Ferrari 512 M 7, 31-38, 43,
 47-49, 62, 101-103, 115-117
Performance; speeds 77-78, 137
Pesch, Franz 29-30
Peterson, Ronnie 27-28, 128
Piëch, Ferdinand 11
Pininfarina design studio 56, 68
Pink Floyd 119
Piper, David 42, 45, 53, 83, 119
Pit stops 111
Pole positions 7, 13, 17-18, 30, 32-33,
 35-36, 47, 104-105, 111, 116, 131, 138
Porsche – *throughout*
 907 40
 908 18, 27, 131; 908L 13; 908 LH 55, 62;
  908/2 18, 22, 27, 134
 910 19
 911 33
 917 – throughout
 917 K 17, 32-33, 40
 917 LH 45, 55, 62
Posey, Sam 18-19, 27-29, 32-33, 35, 38,
 45-49, 55-56, 96, 99-100, 127-131
Power-to-weight ratio 71
Production figure 12, 67-68, 95, 121, 142

Race wins (victories) 7, 15, 18-19, 105, 114,
 125, 129
Read, Steve 138
Redman, Brian 13, 26-27, 96, 134, 137
Regazzoni, Clay 13, 27, 38, 40, 42, 122, 128
Revson, Peter 18-19, 32-35, 37-38, 49,
 131-132

Riverside, Trans-Am race *1970* 100
RM Sotheby's 120-123
 Ferrari Leggenda e Passione auction *2007*
  120; *2008* 125
 Monterey Sports and Classic Car auction
  2007 121
Rocchi, Franco 70
Rodriguez, Pedro 22, 25-27, 30, 35, 38,
 41-43, 47, 98, 100-101, 131
Rodriguez, Riccardo 128
Roschmann, Dieter 143
Rosso, Picchio 22, 128, 142
Royal Automobile Club Belgium 41

Safety roll bars 16, 18, 55, 85
Salt Flat speed trials *1974* 96
Salvarani, Walter 76
Savage, Swede 37-38
SCCA Trans-Am Championship 116; *1969*
 100-101, 103; *1971* 100
Scaglietti, Sergio 66
Scheckter, Jody 107
Schetty, Peter 17-19, 22, 25, 27, 29-30, 128
Schmitz, Herbert 11
Scuderia Brescia Corse 125, 148
Scuderia Filipinetti 25, 27, 32, 40-41, 115,
 128, 142, 152
Scuderia Picchio Rosso 16, 20
Sebring 77, 96, 100, 103
 12-Hours race *1970* 15, 17-19, 105, 119,
  128-129, 131; *1971* 7, 35-38, 49, 101,
  104, 111, 117
Selsdon, Lord 94
Shelby Cobra 10
Sicard, François 57, 77, 89, 96-97, 100, 147
Siffert, Jo 13-14, 20, 22, 25-26, 28-30, 38,
 41-42, 45, 47-48, 131, 134
Silver Flag hill climb, Italy *2011* 143
Silverstone 105, 125, 139
 Classic *2012* 114
 Interserie race *1972* 149; *1974* 151
Solar Productions 118
Spa-Francorchamps 13, 41, 77
 Classic races 124
 Ferrari Days 125
 1,000km race *1970* 26-27, 129, 132;
  1971 41-42
Spare parts 110-111, 116, 122, 133
Sparling, Wayne 16
Spencer, Doane 116
Spencer, Mike 10
Staudenmaier, Herbert 11
Steering 79-81, 130, 137-138
Stommelen, Ralf 38
Stretton, Martin 114
Stroll, Lawrence 117
Summit Point, West Virginia 100-101
Surtees, John 22, 25-27, 128
Surviving cars 121, 125, 142-153
Suspension 34, 79-81, 102, 107
 anti-roll bar 80-81
 coil springs 80, 103
 ride height 81
 shock absorbers 80
 wishbone 80

Swaters, Jacques 26, 29-30, 32, 46, 48, 83,
 128, 132-133 148

Taddei, Mr 55
Targa Florio 47; *1970* 25, 27, 129;
 1971 41
Technical specifications, 512 M and
 512 S 72
Ten Tenths 107
Testing 7, 12, 52-55, 99-100-101, 131
Thruxton RAC Sports Car Championship
 1970 19-20
Tifosi 22, 40, 92
Traco Engineering 105
Transmission 17, 76-78, 110
 clutch 78, 135
 differential 78, 102
 gearbox 71, 76, 78, 100, 107, 135
 gear ratios 76-78
Turin Motor Show *1969* 12
Tyres 78, 83
 Firestone 83
 Goodyear 83

Vaccarella, Nino 17-19, 22, 25-28, 43, 87,
 119, 128, 131-132
Vaccari, William 66
Values 120-124
van Lennep, Gijs 22, 45, 47
Vesty, Paul 19
Vintage Car Stores 115

Walker, Alastair 27, 29
Watkins Glen 96-97, 100
 Can-Am *1971* 49
 6-Hours race *1970* 29-30; *1971* 47-49,
  98, 101, 117, 131
Webb, Ian 118
Weight/weight distribution 12, 54, 56, 62, 66,
 90-91
Weir, David 37, 42
Wheels
 Campagnolo 83
 recommended settings 80
White, Kirk 32, 102-103, 105, 112, 115-117
Wiesendanger, Heinrich 41-42
Williams, Jonathan 134, 146
Wimpffen, János 9, 12
 Time and Two Seats book 31
Wisell, Reine 27-28
Woodard, John 'Woody' 33, 36, 38, 44-45,
 47-48, 78, 100-102, 104, 111, 117
World Manufacturers' Championship 100,
 119-120, 130; *1969* 13, *1970* 29-30; *1971*
 32, 38, 47, 100, 116
Wyer, John 14, 26, 30, 32, 40-41, 47, 104,
 125

Young, Gregg 35, 37-38, 47, 96, 100
Youmg, Irene 37-38

Zeccoli, Teodoro 41
Zeltweg 14, 49, 105
Zolder 77
 Kent 300 Interserie race *1971* 125